GATHER

ALSO BY ASHANTÉ M. REESE

Black Food Geographies: Race, Self-Reliance, and Food Access in Washington, D.C.

Black Food Matters: Racial Justice in the Wake of Food Justice
(coeditor)

NORTON
SHORTS

GATHER

Black Food, Nourishment, and the Art of Togetherness

ASHANTÉ M. REESE

W. W. Norton & Company
Independent and Employee-Owned

Copyright © 2026 by Ashanté M. Reese

All rights reserved
Printed in the United States of America
First Edition

For information about permission to reproduce selections from this
book, write to Permissions, W. W. Norton & Company, Inc.,
500 Fifth Avenue, New York, NY 10110

For information about special discounts for bulk purchases, please
contact W. W. Norton Special Sales at specialsales@wwnorton.com or
800-233-4830

Manufacturing by Lakeside Book Company
Production manager: Delaney Adams

ISBN: 978-1-324-07646-9

W. W. Norton & Company, Inc.
500 Fifth Avenue, New York, NY 10110
www.wwnorton.com

W. W. Norton & Company Ltd.
15 Carlisle Street, London W1D 3BS

Authorized EU representative:
EAS, Mustamäe tee 50, 10621 Tallinn, Estonia

10 9 8 7 6 5 4 3 2 1

To all the grandparents, parents, aunties, uncles, siblings, and cousins who taught me that gathering food—and one another—is sacred work.

And

To Ms. Josephine Searcy and Mr. James Buntin, two members of the Cockrill family featured in Gather, *who passed on before the book was published.*

we are each other's

magnitude and bond.

—"Paul Robeson" by Gwendolyn Brooks

CONTENTS

INTRODUCTION: Why Gather?	1
CHAPTER 1: Gardens	19
CHAPTER 2: Reunions	44
CHAPTER 3: Repasts	72
CHAPTER 4: Mutual Aid	91
CONCLUSION: Gathering on the Brink of Uncertainty	112
ACKNOWLEDGMENTS	119
GATHER: A PLAYLIST	123
NOTES	125
FURTHER READING	135
INDEX	139

GATHER

INTRODUCTION

WHY GATHER?

———

There were two places I could reliably find my grandmother: in her garden or in her kitchen. On countless days, I covered the short distance between her house and mine (we lived next door, with only a narrow ditch separating the properties) to say hi, ask for something to eat, or just be with her. She was that kind of person—the type who drew folks who simply wanted to be near her. I could see or hear her in her garden, stooped over tomatoes or her uncooperative collard greens while talking to the plants or humming a hymn. If there was one constant about my grandmother's garden, it was that she never got her collard or mustard greens to grow the way she wanted, but she tried every season. Witnessing her tend a garden that never quite bent to her will but brought her so much joy taught me that honoring Earth's autonomy is as important as honoring her bounty. Lucky for her, what she couldn't grow herself, others gave freely. She loved it when Mr. Jimmy Pace, who lived maybe ten minutes away, came over with bunches of greens in hand, his gift a salve for the disappointment of her own bad luck with her harvest. Though he never expected it, she'd offer tomatoes or a meal in return—a reciprocity ritual that undergirded everyday life in rural East Texas.

If Mama (as all her grandchildren called her) was in the kitchen, she was cooking something and almost always on the phone while doing it, shushing me as I bolted through her house. Sometimes she was baking cakes, rarely only one. Often, there'd be one for the house and another for a church function or for someone who was sick, bereaved, or in need of a blessing. Being in the kitchen with her while she baked was one of my favorite times, because the reward for watching was the opportunity to lick cake batter from the mixer beaters. Given how impatient I, my younger sister, or cousins who were visiting could be, I doubt it was her favorite! But she never turned us away. In her kitchen and her garden, gathering food was another way to gather strength, dignity, laughter, and herself—amid and despite all the inequities that shaped her life.

A dark-skinned girl-child born seven years before the start of World War II—a war that claimed the lives or minds of many of the men in her community—my grandmother was no stranger to racial and gender violence. She married early because it was customary to do so and spent most of her life working low-wage jobs while taking care of her children and later several of her grandchildren, including me. By any number of metrics, my grandmother would be considered one of the truly disadvantaged. But she was community-minded, creative, and resourceful. As one of my primary caretakers, my grandmother was often responsible for feeding me—dinner after school or sports practice, midday Saturday meals, and breakfast on Sunday mornings before church. When she was pressed for time, she'd make mackerel patties from a can, but the biscuits were often from scratch, which we'd eat with Brer Rabbit syrup, my youngest sister's favorite meal. Watching Mama roll biscuit dough on the countertop with a glass, because she didn't have a baking mat or a rolling pin, taught me that nearly anything could be repurposed to meet our needs.

Not having the proper tools can be evidence of lack, or it can be an invitation to improvise. The difference between lack and improvisation was simply her creativity and tenacity. Whether it was whipping up a meal in the kitchen or tending to the plot of land she cultivated behind her home, the fruits of my grandmother's labor were invitations to learn that being of service with and to others wasn't the same thing as subservience. Instead, these meals and what she was able to grow (or not!) taught me lessons in interdependency. She wove together available ingredients and fed her kin and community with a determined love that nourished our whole beings, which was everything to our formation as humans. Yet she was neither unique nor exceptional in this way. My grandmother, like her mother and her mother's mother, her daughters and now her granddaughters, did the work of gathering. I write (and gather) as part of her legacy.

There are many more stories I could tell you about my grandmother—how she worked as a domestic worker in people's homes and then as a cook at the local elementary school or how the money she made never matched her efforts or the goodness she cultivated in this world. But I won't. My grandmother's story isn't mine to tell, and that isn't my aim here, though it's vital because she introduced me to justice and equity without ever using the words. My grandmother modeled the belief that every person deserves to have their needs met and to be cared for in ways that reflect their autonomy, dignity, and right to be in this world. She offered me and our community more than a hot meal on Sundays and cakes for special occasions. What she and countless others like her offered was nourishment.

It's easy to see a word like "nourishment" and immediately think it means providing food or sustenance that is good for the physical body. That is one definition of nourishment, but there is so much more to the sacred practice of caring for oneself and others. In fact, many definitions of the word "nourish" emphasize tending to or cultivating a person's needs beyond sustenance, which suggests that the act of nourishing ourselves and one another is much bigger than providing food. For example, I bake a blackberry cobbler, or berry pie as we called it growing up, every year on June 18, my grandmother's birthday. It's a tradition I started when she passed away in 2014. At first, it was about honoring her memory, as I tried to perfect a dish that means a lot to me. Every year, I gather fresh blackberries. I roll out dough on my countertop the way she did it, using a glass instead of a rolling pin. I practice different types of lattice tops, my own spin on this sacred dish.

Initially, this ritual was one I kept to myself. But in the past ten years, it has rippled outward. I still prepare it alone, but I share the cobbler with others, sometimes telling stories of my grandmother along with the offering. I've done this with other foods: learning to make teacakes from my mother, because when I was in graduate school she'd mail them to me, crafting a vegan version of Southern dressing for Friendsgivings so that no one would feel left out of the culture. In each of these scenarios food is present, but so is the desire to honor ancestors, uplift cultural traditions, and cultivate intimacy. On any other day, a cobbler may be just a cobbler. But on my grandmother's birthday, in the presence of friends who witness how I honor her, it's transformed into something that nourishes my entire being; a collective, communal affair.

That combination of food and community is what I take away from my grandmother's efforts and from my own attempts to create conditions for nourishment in my communities. Nourishment is bigger than what we eat, and it starts before we ever offer or consume food. Perhaps that is one of the most counterintuitive things to take in—that if we truly care about nourishing physical bodies, we first have to commit to nourishing whole people. That starts with values like building community across difference, equitably sharing resources, building trust such that you believe others enter spaces with good intentions, and prioritizing caring for others over competition. These and similar values show up in the gatherings I focus on in this book: in garden spaces, at repasts and reunions, and within mutual aid efforts.

These values form the foundation on which we can and should build movements around food. Thus, the first thing I want you to consider as we journey in this book together is this: we've been taught one thing about nourishment—that it means to feed the physical body—but nourishment is also about tending to the social body. This is where *Gather* enters: an exploration of how to marry the lessons about gathering from my grandmother with our visions for food justice. This is an invitation to broaden our understanding of what nourishment means and how it can look.

IF YOU'RE ANYTHING LIKE ME, ideas about nourishment and phrases like "food justice" weren't a part of your vocabulary growing up. Even with the early experiences in my grandmother's kitchen that taught me about the role of food in building and sustaining community, I rarely thought about food as something political. This changed after seeing the urgent, immediate inequalities I saw when I moved away from my small town in East Texas.

My first concrete lessons in food inequity came from eleven- and twelve-year-olds. When I finished my undergraduate degree, I moved to Atlanta to teach at Coretta Scott King Young Women's Leadership Academy, a predominantly Black single-gender public school that was founded the year I joined the teaching staff. Most of our students came from neighborhoods that had some of the highest poverty and crime rates in the city. They also experienced some of the highest rates of food insecurity and had the least access to fresh, healthy food—a trend that persists, according to a 2023 study conducted by Megan Winkler and her colleagues at Emory University's Rollins School of Public Health. On one occasion, I took a few students to a grocery store and then served them dinner at my home. While we sat at the dining room table together, they changed the whole trajectory of my life by simply pointing out that the food they had access to in their neighborhood was significantly inferior to what I had in my neighborhood less than five miles away. Those students asked a number of questions: *Why does your neighborhood have the nice grocery stores? Why do you have so many more kinds of fruits and vegetables than we do?* They also had critiques: *It's like they don't care if we have options.* and *How are we supposed to eat healthy if everything around us is unhealthy?* Gathered around a table on a random school night, we mused about what it means to be healthy, to feel confident and nourished, to feel included in society.

Their questions became my questions, and their critiques were guideposts for my own curiosity when I returned to graduate school to study anthropology. I became obsessed with learning how cities work, and how macro-level forces shape the everyday realities of people like my students and their families. I took an internship at the Johns Hopkins Center for Health Disparities Solutions to understand the relationship between residential segregation and health outcomes, and I sought mentorship from sociologists who were experts in urban design and inequities. I learned that my students' observations were not an anomaly. Predominantly Black urban neighborhoods in the US, regardless of income, have fewer food resources than their white counterparts. As I'd learn, this lack of provisioning has major impacts on long-term health. Sometimes referred to as obesogenic environments, neighborhoods with less access to fresh produce and grocery stores, or that lack sidewalks and green space, are risk factors for obesity, diabetes, and hypertension. When people have easier access to fast-food chains and liquor stores than grocery stores or farmers markets, that impacts the decisions people make about what they'll eat.

For example, my middle school students in Atlanta could walk to a corner store with burglar bars on the window or a fast-food restaurant in the same amount of time it would take me to reach my choice of four grocery stores. Relatedly, many of their parents worked long hours and weekends, making time a factor in how and when they shopped for groceries. In contrast, while I was in graduate school, I supported myself by babysitting for wealthy families in the Washington, D.C., area. After school, there was one place that these kids always wanted to go: McDonald's. There was one place that parents almost always said it was okay for me to take them: McDonald's. These kids, mostly wealthy and mostly white, were never the poster children of the childhood obesity epidemic. They weren't the imagined victims of the fast-food industry. They, unlike the students I taught in Atlanta, were just kids with choices.

What I learned from these experiences was that there wasn't anything inherently different about the kind of choices kids would make if given the opportunity. The main difference was the range of choices they had. For my students, that landscape was limited. The experiences of my students directly challenged the myth that poor people and people of color are more inclined toward unhealthy foods. Instead, the structures that shaped their world—the facts that healthy grocery stores were farther away, their parents often worked overtime at low-wage jobs, and fast food was the least expensive option—funneled them toward foods that weren't the healthiest options.

To convey that these problems are structural and not caused by individual choices, activists and scholars use the term "food apartheid," which they define as the system of racialized inequality in food access. The idea of food apartheid forces us to zoom out and consider how many systems are deliberately built to work against certain consumers based on race and geography. Karen Washington, longtime food justice activist and cofounder of Black Urban Growers (BUGs), plainly stated that food apartheid "looks at the whole system, along with race, geography, faith, and economics. You say 'food apartheid' and you get to the root cause of some of the problems around the food system. It brings in hunger and poverty. It brings us to the more important question: What are some of the social inequities that you see, and what are you doing to erase some of the injustices?" This question is at the heart of the food justice movement, a movement that aims to expose inequalities that shape our food world and to work toward equity.

Food justice has received a lot of attention and support over the past twenty-five years, though its origins are arguably much older. Some point to the Black Panther Party's Free Breakfast for Children program and Fannie Lou Hamer's Freedom Farms Collective in Sunflower County, Mississippi, in the 1960s as early experiments that formed a foundation for the food justice movement. In *Food Justice*, the first full-length book about the subject, published in 2010, Robert Gottlieb, cofounder of the Urban and Environmental Policy Institute at Occidental College, and Anupama Joshi, cofounder of the National Farm to School Network, characterized food justice as "ensuring that the benefits and risks of where, what, and how food is grown and produced, transported and distributed, and accessed and eaten are shared fairly." Inherent in their definition is a sense of shared fate—a counter to a version of food consumption that overemphasizes individual choice. Gottlieb and Joshi helped us understand that a justice orientation toward food requires us to shift the benefits and risks such that the blessings and burdens are more equitably shared. Many organizations and researchers have built on this approach, with most diagnosing the problems in the food system as stemming from the prioritization of profits over people's well-being while also providing direct aid and access to impacted communities. For over fifteen years, I've witnessed this work in real time. In D.C., the Green Scheme established gardens at housing projects so that residents could build self-sufficiency. At one location where I was researching, one of the residents would pick whatever was left in the garden to make a huge pot of soup to share with others when money was low. In Atlanta, a group of Black farmers founded the Southwest Atlanta Growers Cooperative (SWAG) to provide more produce in southwest Atlanta. All over the country,

I've encountered individuals and organizations who haven't waited for food environments to change on their own. Instead, they've set out to change things themselves.

What was once a grassroots movement rooted in principles that emphasized growing community control over food systems is now firmly mainstream, with thousands of organizations across the country. Mainstream means more people listening, more people paying attention to the problem, more opportunities to address the inequalities we so desperately want to eradicate. But there's also a risk for co-optation, with the most radical components of the movement being sidelined because of either pragmatism (prioritizing the work that can get funded) or discomfort. For the early architects, food was always political and thus, so too was food justice—a direct affront to unfair systems. But as the movement has grown, what is considered justice in regard to food is increasingly nebulous. Sometimes, the urgency of providing healthy food eclipses the equally important need to build new infrastructures such that one day, food inequalities will no longer exist. That is a huge, daunting task that won't happen overnight. But we can't lose sight of it even as we meet the needs of communities who require immediate support.

There's also a risk that those who are creating visions for what they believe food justice is do so without relationships with or input from the communities they want to serve. This disconnect might prioritize "healthy food" while wholly missing the mark on the reality that justice is a collaborative effort that must include vision and leadership from the communities being served. As food justice has firmly taken its place in the mainstream, "food" and "justice" aren't always in alignment. In fact, sometimes they're at odds. Radical dreams also cost a lot of money and require a lot of effort. But what if the challenges we face are invitations to redefine where and how we seek value?

In almost every class I teach, I tell students that part of what we're experiencing in an unjust food system is a crisis of scale. Our current, corporatized food system prioritizes increasing size and reach, consolidation, monopolization, and standardization not only across the country but across the world. The industrialized food system is too big and requires inequality to sustain itself. The challenge with scaling up is that the bigger the scale at which something operates, the harder it is to infuse it with values that everyday people espouse and the harder it is to make it accountable for the lives it touches. On the other side of the equation, the further away something is from people's bodies and lived experiences, the harder it is for them to imagine that they can have any impact on it. The produce in our grocery basket is often grown across the world, picked by people we'll never meet in places we'll never go, and the problems of hunger and access seem unimaginably vast. Even if we wanted to change these systems, where would we start?

Thinking at a large scale can feel overwhelming. Luckily for us, that isn't the only register at which we can find inspiration or practice our values. Our everyday lives present unlimited opportunities to construct justice and liberation in our food system and otherwise. No matter the size of the action, the point is that liberation doesn't just happen. We have to work toward it in everything we do. If nothing else, *that* is what I hope you learn from the people and gatherings in this book. The values we practice and the rituals we build in our everyday lives hold keys to how to transform our food system. People like my grandmother understood the power of togetherness. We must take the lessons they offer us more seriously.

GATHER IS AN EFFORT to bring those early lessons in nourishment that I gleaned from my grandmother and home community together with everything I've learned about food justice over the past fifteen years. Where can we look for fresh inspiration as we continue to imagine a liberated food system and liberated lives? What would it look like if we espouse a more expansive definition of nourishment? What would we have to let go of? What would we need to cling to? Without government funding and programs that place justice at the center, can we still build the (food) worlds we want to see? These are some of the questions I grapple with daily. The answers aren't neat or easy, but I think we're closer to them than we think. One of the core arguments of this book is that everyday ways people get together to meet the physical and social needs of others make up a masterclass for how to hone the values that are less quantifiable. Who better to learn from than the experts themselves—everyday people who put nourishment into practice as a way of life.

It is imperative that we put nourishment at the center of food justice movements. We can take inspiration from organizations like the National Black Food and Justice Alliance (NBFJA), which is leading some of the most exciting, expansive work right now, ranging from offering direct support to Black farmers to establishing centers for the study and practice of Afroecology at historically Black colleges and universities (HBCUs). Each year, they celebrate this work with an annual gathering, an event that nourishes everyone to continue the arduous work of building better infrastructures. We must also take inspiration from everyday people like those featured in this book. It is a loving calling in, an invitation for us to reconsider what we are fighting for, how we're fighting for those things, and how those people's knowledge and ways of being are embedded in our visions for the future. I'm not saying our food justice movements have failed. I'm saying we're at an impasse, and we've got to look beyond the echo chambers that currently define what is important and what is at stake.

I turn toward Black gatherings to reframe our understanding of what is possible in the food world, by looking at what is already happening when Black people gather around food. It is an attempt to write about a belief I hold deeply, a belief that has held me deeply: there is no inherent deficit in Black people. In fact, if we look closely enough, if we are curious enough, much of the magic and creativity that happens when Black people gather can be transformative not only for us but for the entire world. *Gather* starts from the premise that death, destruction, and denial are not the only ways to index Black life. By looking at the spaces where Black people gather, we can also witness the beauty of Black aliveness—in all its goodness, contradictions, love, and capaciousness.

In early 2023, I put out a call for people to share their experiences with Black gatherings, inviting them to participate in any of six ways: sit for an oral history interview; invite me to a family reunion; submit memories or stories about reunions, repasts, or communal experiences with gardening or food organizing; submit family reunion memorabilia (flyers, buttons, T-shirts, etc.); submit photos or videos of personal family gatherings; or submit recipes. Sixty-one people responded, and almost thirty of them included invitations to family reunions. During the summer of 2023, I went to six of them—including my own family reunion that I had not attended in over ten years. I invited participants at the reunions I could not join to share reflections, images, and audio through my website. In addition to attending the reunions, I conducted fifteen oral history interviews with people whom I didn't meet in person.

People offered photos of celebrations, recipes, flyers advertising family reunions, stories about barbecues and potlucks, and memories. Others sat for interviews where they shared stories about their family rituals with me. In exchange, I had those interviews transcribed and gave them the audio and the transcript—an investment in their family's archive. This multimodal approach not only expanded my ethnographic reach but also allowed people to reflect on their own experience with gathering without it being mediated by my questions or presence. In total, the people who responded to my call contributed over three hundred artifacts to this project, alongside the many hours people spent sharing their stories. Not all those stories and artifacts show up in this book, but the spirit of what was shared is very much threaded through these pages.

When I turned to exploring what gatherings can teach us about food justice, I thought it appropriate to return home—to the people, places, and practices that created the foundation for my current work. I wanted to return to rituals and experiences that I know intimately to see if I could look at them anew and glean some inspiration for food justice. I was guided by the notion that perhaps what we're looking for already lives among us. Like renowned Black anthropologist Zora Neale Hurston, who returned to her hometown, Eatonville, as a source of anthropological inspiration, I returned to mine, to write as an insider, a person who has a stake in the game, a daughter of the very spaces and practices that show up throughout this book. Instead of sitting from a distance, I write from up close, choosing to focus on rituals and practices that have transformed my own life, because I believe they hold keys for how to broaden our understanding of nourishment. I do so with curiosity and humility, but I make no claims of objectivity. I have a vested interest in bringing together the joys and challenges of Black gatherings with questions of how to fortify our food justice movements. Bringing more of myself into this writing, alongside the stories and experiences of others I met during fieldwork, means I write from a position of "we." This doesn't mean I speak for others or that we're all the same. But "we" is a powerful place from which to claim kinship and community—a place where I understand that my well-being, my life, and my nourishment are intimately bound to that of others. Being part of a "we" is a form of care that recognizes the shared risks and rewards of being together.

As an anthropologist, I sift, weigh, and find value in what people say as well as what they don't say about what matters most to them in the food system. My dear friend, collaborator, and fellow anthropologist Hanna Garth has offered "the politics of adequacy" as one way to understand how communities' desires, preferences, and values factor into their food choices. She posed the following questions: "What makes a provisioning system adequate? And adequate to what ends?" These questions force us to consider what exactly we are fighting for. Is it access? Is it a standardized version of healthiness? Is it people's right to live a fully nourished, healthy life—of which food is only one dimension? And I would add a question that I think is deeply challenging to those of us who are interested in food and justice: Adequate to *whose* ends? What do we do with different, sometimes competing visions of what it means to live a good, decent life? For those of us interested in these questions, where might we turn? I'd like to suggest that we turn to practices that aren't easy to measure but which meaningfully contribute to what we call "equity" and "justice": gardening, family reunions, repasts, and mutual aid.

The themes explored in this book emerge from a very simple set of questions: What can we learn from how Black people gather around food? What kinds of practices nourish us on an individual and community level? And, because I spend much of my life thinking about where food and justice intersect, what can food justice movements learn from community-centered practices that feature food as a significant component? These questions are rooted in the legacy of all that I learned from my grandmother and the communities who raised me.

FOR A LONG TIME, the dirt road I grew up on was not on any map. To the outside world it did not exist, and by extension neither did we. And yet we practiced generosity, care, and what I might now call radical community-building, which made it possible for us to leave our doors unlocked, to take seriously the mandate to take good care of one another, and to be together through beauty and catastrophe. It was the first place I experienced freedom: being allowed to wander as long as I wanted, being encouraged to follow blackberry vines and pick the fruit that would be transformed into pies and cobblers by my grandmother. This goodness did not change the fact that the dirt road was unimproved in part because of anti-Black racism—the paved highway stopped where Blackness began. It did not change the fact that because of this, when it rained, the road flooded and we had to make a calculated decision on whether leaving was worth getting stuck in the mud. It did not change the fact that most of us were poor. But what that road—what the community that thrived along it—did offer us was nourishment, a living experiment in practicing freedom within enclosure. I'm still mining those garden and kitchen lessons. They are compasses for my activism and my way of being in the world. I hope the ones I share from my grandmother and communities across the country become compasses for you too.

Gather is an offering to anyone who wants to feel connected to the power of being there for others. In our world, building community around gardening or organizing yearly family reunions is often taken for granted. Yet nothing has revolutionized my life more profoundly than tuning in to these acts, these steady insistences that announce to the world that we are here and intend to remain. There is a scripture that I return to often when I think about what happens when Black people gather around food: "For where two or three gather in my name, there am I with them." I am not particularly religious, and *Gather* is not a religious text. But the spirit of this passage leaves an impression on me. So, for our journey through various kinds of Black gatherings, I am revising that scripture to say: When two or three gather in the name of care, connection, and service, there is freedom with them.

Reader, this also isn't a cookbook. Sure, there is food. Tons of it. Who can have a family reunion without chicken or barbecue, or a repast without countless sweets? But food isn't the center. The values, epistemologies, and ways of being that undergird Black life are the heart. I hope that centering those things helps us see food and the food justice movement differently. Consider this book an invitation—a personal invitation—to be curious, hopeful, and even a bit skeptical about what gardens, reunions, and repasts have to do with justice. By the time you put it down, I hope you're inspired to rethink the scale and pace of transformation, and the wonder of food itself as an archive and a connector within the social body which is necessary for our collective survival. Bonus: Perhaps—for the uninitiated—you will also understand why you should never, ever, show up to a Black gathering empty-handed. We all have something to offer. But please, for goodness' sake, if you have not been bestowed the honor of bringing the potato salad, just . . . don't.

CHAPTER 1

GARDENS

―――

Pleasant Hope Baptist is not a large church. Set back from the street, nestled among rowhouses and two or three businesses in north Baltimore, it looks like a lot of urban Black churches: brick exterior and a marquee out front with the church's name and a message for the week. Though I lived in Baltimore in 2019 and part of 2020, I had never visited the church or its garden until June 2023. But I had met Reverend Dr. Heber Brown III at a conference; he was the main champion of starting the church's garden, and I was inspired by the congregation's work to reimagine the church's role in food security.

I was no stranger to church involvement in alleviating food insecurity. I grew up in and around Black churches. When I was in college, I worked as a receptionist at a church that housed a weekly food pantry. That church was one of many; nearly half of the churches and other faith-based organizations in the US report organizing some kind of food distribution program. But doing so through gardening, farmers markets held at the church, and connecting congregants directly to Black farmers as Pleasant Hope was doing was revolutionary. At Pleasant Hope, the goal was not only to feed people but to also sow seeds of self-determination such that the community could see an alternative to depending on the corporate-controlled food system.

I thought about my early impressions of Heber as I arrived at Pleasant Hope Baptist to tour the church and its legendary garden for the first time. I had met Heber four years earlier, in 2019, at the annual Black Urban Growers and Farmers (BUGs) conference in New York City, where he was the keynote speaker. Then, he was Pleasant Hope's pastor and a celebrity in Black-led food justice spaces—not because he solved hunger, not because he was a politician who made big promises, but because of how his pastoral work had blossomed into a larger movement. Heber was the founder and executive director of the Black Church Food Security Network (BCFSN), a national network of over 250 Black churches committed to building health, wealth, and power in their communities. When he stepped up to the podium at BUGs—and before offering sermonic remarks on the legacy and promise of Black farming traditions, in an auditorium of Black people from many faith traditions—Heber broke out into a smile and a church song. We clapped, and clapped some more, and rocked side to side as he sang, "We will shout and sing God's praise / Everybody will be happy over there." Between the earnest way he connected faith and farming, his singing, and his warm personality, the audience was captivated.

As soon as I got out of my car in front of Pleasant Hope, Heber jumped out of his red Ford pickup across the street, sporting what I'd come to know as his characteristic smile. It is damn near impossible not to smile back at him. He is modest, unimposing, and leads with curiosity. He's the kind of person who you can tell is a good listener just by looking at him. Being around him makes me want to be a good listener too. He was wearing a shirt with Fannie Lou Hamer's face and name on it, underneath which was written "Rebel." From my years following his work I knew he was a student of Black women's leadership and labor, and every chance he got he made sure to uplift their legacies.

Heber led me through a waist-high wire-linked gate that separated the garden from the street. If someone wanted to, they could hop right over the fence and into the garden. There were no privacy bushes, or the other barriers that often divide private space and those who have no right to it. It was a weekday afternoon, not primetime gardening hours. Besides Heber and me, no one else was there. Taking up about 1,500 square feet in front of the church, the garden was composed of a dozen raised beds. In the center, four of them intersected in a cross. There was not much growing. In fact, it looked like there hadn't been much effort put into the garden at all, despite it being summer, one of the peak growing periods in Baltimore. But on average, this garden produced about 1,200 pounds of food each year, mostly cucumbers, broccoli, kale, tomatoes, and corn. Not a bad yield for the small space, but even as someone who believes in the magic of small, everyday-scale interventions, it was hard for me to wrap my head around how such a tiny plot started a whole movement. Heber began his tour by showing me the first beds he built in 2010 and telling me what preceded them in the garden's story: the words, admonitions, and vision of a Black woman, Mama Maxine.

When Heber came to pastor Pleasant Hope, he was twenty-eight years old. The next youngest person in church leadership was sixty-three. A third-generation pastor, Heber was no stranger to church politics or to the delicate balance between leading a congregation and listening to them. But he quickly learned there was still a lot for him to figure out. Heber was committed to the vision of Pleasant Hope being a church invested in social justice and Black empowerment. To that end, he envisioned bold new programs: gardening, summer freedom schools for young people, and other programs that subverted the charity models that are central to many church ministries. They'd done things a particular way at Pleasant Hope. Then came this new pastor with ideas for how the church could be involved in the community in unconventional ways—or, at least, ways they weren't used to. Soon enough, a couple of senior members organized a meeting after one Sunday service to address their concerns. Some said they had no confidence in the young pastor. Heber just sat in the pulpit and listened. Finally, Mama Maxine, a longtime member and elder, stood and said, "I don't know why y'all mess with Pastor Brown. He's the best pastor we've ever had, and you should be ashamed of yourselves for giving him so much trouble." After Mama Maxine spoke, the meeting ended.

Although Mama Maxine and others defended Heber, he still listened to the criticisms and took responsibility for the tension: "I had all these ideas for programs and plans for all kinds of stuff, but what about the people right in front of me?" Heber wisely understood that a leader with no followers is just a person shouting ideas into a void. If Pleasant Hope was going to become more involved in the community, Heber was going to have to move at the speed of trust. He'd earned the trust of Mama Maxine, but he had work to do with others. In the meantime, her trust in him bolstered his confidence, and his apprenticeship with her would be vital to establishing the garden that he felt was urgently needed.

One of the social issues Heber wanted to prioritize was food security. When he became pastor, one in five people in Baltimore—about 125,000 people—lived in neighborhoods that were classified as food deserts: the closest supermarket was more than a quarter mile away, over 40 percent of households did not have a car, and the median household income was at or below 185 percent of the federal poverty level. The USDA Food Access Research Atlas allows users to enter addresses into a map to understand the food environment residents live in. When I typed in Pleasant Hope's address, the church was surrounded by swaths of forest green and orange—indicating that residents near the church were either far from a grocery store (green) or had low incomes and poor transportation options (orange).

Like many others, Heber was concerned about the impact of the food environment on his congregation specifically and Baltimore's Black communities in general. Black people comprise more than 60 percent of Baltimore's population and carry a disproportionate burden of food insecurity and obesity, in large part because they are more economically disadvantaged than their white neighbors. Heber saw an opportunity to address both food and economic inequalities, but it would require ushering his congregation into a more expansive understanding of ministry, starting with getting comfortable talking about how white supremacy shapes Black communities and individual lives.

Heber wanted to build a garden and a network of food distribution that the whole community could benefit from. Pleasant Hope's garden was a response to modern problems—food insecurity and diet-related illnesses—but it was rooted in a storied Black agrarian tradition of Black people in the Americas working within social, economic, and geographical constraints to envision and create fuller versions of their lives. During enslavement, Black people across the African Diaspora often managed their own plots near their dwellings. Plantation owners expected enslaved people to supplement their diets, and sometimes the meals of those in the main house, with whatever they grew. In some cases, enslaved people were also able to sell their produce. For example, Bagwell and Minerva Granger, who were enslaved at Thomas Jefferson's Monticello, fed their nine children from their personal garden and likely sold produce to Jefferson's relatives. Plantation owners may have seen these personal gardens as merely bonus income, but the enslaved themselves saw much more through their imaginations and hopes for the future. These plots were not only spaces to gather food—they were also spaces to gather one another.

Specifically, these gardens created a way for enslaved Black people to maintain cultural ties and affirm their values. They cultivated plants and herbs that they had brought from Africa, including okra and yam, as one way to remain connected to their homeland. For special events like birthdays, weddings, and births, the bounty of these small plots was used in service of celebration. Traditional values that ran counter to chattel slavery, including communalism, respecting elders, and honoring the sacredness of Earth, lived on through these gardening practices. With meager tools and borrowed time, under the ever-present vigilance of plantation surveillance, enslaved Black people improvised lives that were shaped by chattel slavery but not entirely defined by it. These plots provided space for ingenuity, care, creativity, and expressions of love.

These practices of autonomy and cultural preservation are what cultural theorist Sylvia Wynter has called "cultural guerrilla resistance." Wynter wrote that for the enslaved person who had been ripped from her homeland, "the land remained the Earth—and the

Earth was a goddess; man used the land to feed himself; and to offer first fruits to the Earth; . . . Around the growing of yam, of food for survival, he created on the plot a folk culture—the basis of a social order—in three hundred years." It is one thing to feed oneself. It is an entirely different thing to understand the life-giving power of what the Earth provides such that it is the center of an entire social order.

The survival of people, food, and traditions is no trifling matter. It is, in fact, one of the most remarkable feats that connects people across the African Diaspora. The tale of okra, in its journey from West Africa to the United States, is one amazing example of how Black people have fought for the survival of their food and traditions. As the story goes, African women who anticipated being sold into slavery braided okra seeds into their hair so that they could plant them in the new world. From Ghanaian okra stew to Louisiana gumbo and its seafood-heavy derivative in Maryland, okra's journey from West Africa to the United States highlights how the sheer will to preserve has sustained cultural connections over centuries. Okra has become a point of connection for Black people across the world. It's also an example that should animate how we think about food justice. Where there is survival, there are also strategies and forms of gathering that can inform—and perhaps improve—our quest for justice. Despite how much I loathe okra (seriously, you can take my Black card, that's how much I dislike it), I respect what it teaches me about nourishment.

Stories like these—about the history of vegetables like okra, the role of gardens and farms in cultural preservation, and the faith required to root yourself in a pursuit of liberation—animated Heber's arguments about the value of a garden at Pleasant Hope Baptist Church. Heber prepared his congregation for a garden and activism like a community organizer. He studied other preachers who had mobilized their congregations around food, such as Vernon Johns, who preceded Dr. Martin Luther King Jr. as pastor of Dexter Avenue Baptist Church in Montgomery, Alabama, and who is sometimes called the father of the civil rights movement. One of the hallmarks of Reverend Johns's ministry was his belief that land ownership and farming were key to Black economic freedom. In an essay published in 1933, Johns put forth a vision of how growing food could unite rural and urban Black folks in pursuit of greater autonomy: "Urban and rural Negroes working together could control the production of their elemental necessities on the farm and become merchants of those in the city. It is apparent also, that several new avenues to employment would be opened by this enterprise." His politics weren't easily accepted by his middle-class Black congregants, many of whom were hesitant to align themselves with farming—something that they believed was a step backward. Much to their dismay, Johns, a farmer himself, pressed forward in his convictions, sometimes selling produce outside the church on Sundays—a practice that Heber himself would adopt and expand into markets at the church.

Fannie Lou Hamer was another of Heber's muses. A Black woman born in 1917, Hamer was a sharecropper who was evicted from the farm where she worked for attempting to register to vote. Rather than consider this a setback, Hamer saw it as an invitation. Though she would come to be known mostly for her political organizing around voting, declaring that she was "sick and tired of being sick and tired," her work made it clear that controlling one's food system was as urgent a political matter as voting.

As a former sharecropper, Hamer knew the ways food was used as a tool of white supremacy. In 1962, an all-white board of supervisors in nearby Leflore County, Mississippi, voted to discontinue the county's participation in the Federal Surplus Food Commodity Program, a program that the majority Black and poor citizenship depended on. In the wake of the vote, which is referred to as the Greenwood Food Blockade, more than 20,000 Black farmers and sharecroppers were left without reliable food provisioning. Well into the spring of 1963, Hamer witnessed the hunger and panic that many Black folks experienced as a result. Some saw the Greenwood Food Blockade as retaliation for the efforts of the Student Nonviolent Coordinating Committee (SNCC), a radical civil rights organization that challenged segregation in places like Mississippi. To alleviate suffering and fear, SNCC and Hamer organized a national food drive and distributed free food to those impacted by the blockade.

Witnessing how those in power used food to intimidate and manipulate people no doubt fueled Hamer's determination. She envisioned thwarting that control by building a different kind of power, what historian Bobby Smith II called emancipatory food power—a vision of food as central to liberation. "Down where we are, food is used as a political weapon," Hamer reasoned. "But if you have a pig in your backyard, if you have some vegetables in your garden, you can feed yourself and your family and nobody can push you around." With a $10,000 donation, Hamer purchased forty acres to start Freedom Farms Cooperative in Sunflower County, Mississippi, in the late 1960s, which would grow thousands of pounds of okra, tomatoes, collard greens, peas, corn, and other vegetables to feed over 1,500 families. Hamer gathered anyone who wanted to work toward liberation by tending the land together. Black people, white people, poor people—no one was turned away.

Even though there had been some progress since Johns's and Hamer's times, the food system in Baltimore was still shaped by institutional racism, and Heber saw a need for emancipatory food power that could help his community. As Heber followed the north star formed by his predecessors, he also studied scripture, piecing together a vision for the kind of preacher and leader he wanted to be. He started to see himself in the tradition of John the Baptist. In biblical tales, John the Baptist's approach to reaching people was radical. Rather than seek them out in the temples, he called people into the wilderness. Instead of praising their willingness to meet him there, he admonished them to not think too highly of themselves. When the crowd gathered around him, he told them that repenting was not enough; their actions needed to reflect their redemption. They asked how, and he replied: "Anyone who has two shirts should share with the one who has none, and anyone who has food should do the same." Heber, a young preacher armed with lessons from Vernon Johns, Fannie Lou Hamer, and John the Baptist, called his congregation into the wilderness. Luckily for them, the wilderness wasn't far. It was right in the church's front yard.

Heber began by preaching this plan in his sermons, challenging the notion that gardening is a hobby or merely a great weekend activity. It can be those things, of course, but Heber asked his congregation to consider how gardening was connected to the practice of their faith and the commandments to love thy neighbor as thyself, to be of charity to others, and to be good stewards of the blessings bestowed upon them. Growing food, he urged, was an imperative and another sanctuary for their expression of worship and desire to connect with community. From the pulpit, he'd tell stories about church members he visited in hospitals, how they were suffering from diet-related conditions that could be prevented or reversed with proper nutrition. He shared how Hamer and Johns used food as a means toward building sovereignty. In one sermon, he shared a story about visiting Belvedere Square—a retail space about two blocks from the church, with multiple restaurants ranging from Thai to pizza and a storefront for a family-owned farm that sold meat, cheeses, and butter—and reeling at the high food prices. He wasn't saying anything the congregants didn't know. Everyone who'd ever been to Belvedere Square knew that the high prices were one way to signal who belonged there and who didn't. But coming from the pulpit, the message was validating, affirming many congregants' belief that Belvedere Square had not been built with them in mind.

Heber saw his sermons as a form of storytelling, which he extended to the weekly church bulletin. "I treated [the newsletter] like the *New York Times*," he told me with laughter. "Planting seeds and telling the stories every week—especially because some of the most amazing things happened during the week when most of the congregation wasn't there." One of the stories he told was about a woman who had lived across from the church for thirty years but had never visited. One day, when she saw Heber and others working in the garden, she came across the street to offer gardening tools to support their efforts. From her post as an observer, she saw the significance of the work that the church was doing, and Heber saw her investment as a sign to keep going.

He also developed a sixteen-week political education course, something that isn't typical of churches. Political education—collective study that often radically departs from mainstream education—has been a tool of radical Black organizations for decades. The Black Panther Party, for example, taught children Black history and class awareness that wasn't taught in school and encouraged literacy through letter-writing campaigns to political prisoners—all while they fed the kids breakfast. The Black Panther Party's practice of pairing political education with community meals was one of Heber's inspirations. Though his methods were uncharacteristic of many churches, Heber saw this course as another form of discipleship. He was not alone. Thirty congregants joined. Each week, Heber paired scripture with readings about Black history and current events, inviting participants to think together about the congregation's responsibility in an unjust world.

Still, congregants had concerns about starting the garden. Church ministries, traditionally, were Bible study, choirs, food pantries, and the like. Some wondered if the garden was necessary, and others worried that it might draw unnecessary attention to the church, specifically from the FBI or other government agencies that have a history of surveilling "radical" Black organizing and politics. They also wondered what dangers they might be bringing upon themselves by challenging white power structures in the city and beyond. Their concerns weren't misplaced. From the 1963 bombing of the 16th Street Baptist Church in Birmingham, Alabama, that killed four Black girls to the 2015 terrorist attack that killed nine people at Mother Emanuel AME Church in Charleston, South Carolina, Black churches haven't been immune to white supremacist violence—and sometimes have been the specific targets of it. What would Pleasant Hope risk by putting themselves on others' radar? Congregants also worried about Heber himself, and some suggested that he needed security. Whether they knew it or not, their concerns revealed that they had come to realize the power of growing food: the power to build self-determination and provide alternatives to mainstream food outlets. They recognized that growing food could be seen as a threat to the status quo. That wasn't just or fair—but it was the devil they knew.

Despite the anxieties and despite some resistance, Pleasant Hope's garden was officially founded—blessed and prayed over—in April 2010, the culminating event of Earth Week.

HEBER FACED MORE THAN safety concerns from the congregation; there were also practical challenges to starting a garden. First, there was the question of where the garden would live. Heber thought they needed more space than the church had, so he began scouting for plots to buy or lease. Mama Maxine told him no, they had everything they needed right there. "I had this thought that we needed a whole lot of land to make an impact," Heber reflected. "But her leadership in this space and the ways in which she was able to lead us in growing 1,200 pounds of produce per year taught me you don't need a whole lot of space."

Mama Maxine was teaching Heber to be a savvy land steward. She was also drawing on a long tradition of Black farmers who learned to navigate an unjust agricultural landscape that continuously undermined their efforts at self-determination. Since the time of slavery, Black people in the US have encountered systemic efforts to thwart their land ownership. After Emancipation, land ownership was a priority for many African Americans, who collectively amassed about 15 million acres by 1910. However, since then, more than 90 percent of that land has been lost due to theft and discrimination. In Maryland, Black farmers operated 5,859 farms in 1900, compared to

40,169 operated by white farmers. Half a century later, that number had decreased to 3,595 and continued to dwindle because of both discrimination and the pressures to modernize that made farming a challenge for many, regardless of race. In recognition of the systemic dispossession of Black farmers, Senators Cory Booker, Elizabeth Warren, and Kirsten Gillibrand introduced the Justice for Black Farmers Act in 2020 to, in part, restore land that Black farmers had lost due to discrimination.

While securing land is generally difficult, there are particular challenges for those who want to grow food in cities. Across the US, residents have transformed city-owned vacant lots into gardens and farms, with or without permission, turning liabilities into assets for their communities. Mostly, cities have endorsed this idea, because residents adopting vacant lots means less responsibility for the city to develop or police those spaces. For residents, these gardens allow them to take ownership of their communities and practice autonomy. But those arrangements are tenuous. At any moment, a city-owned parcel of land can be taken back or sold, leaving those who may have invested years cultivating it with very little recourse. So, when Mama Maxine suggested growing on the church's land, she was encouraging Heber not only to tap into what was available but to provide some measure of security.

Once Heber committed to cultivating the garden, he had a lot to learn. Though he had a vision, he had few gardening skills. Mama Maxine became his teacher and hype woman in a church hat. An elder who grew up with eight brothers and sisters on a farm in Roanoke Rapids, North Carolina, Mama Maxine knew a thing or two about growing food. She taught her young pastor many of the basics. Heber learned, for example, how to interplant different crops to maximize space. Lettuce might be planted under taller plants like pole beans, because lettuce does not mind the shade. Similarly, companion planting involves placing plants in proximity to protect against pests or improve pollination—for example, marigolds deter pests from nearby cucumbers, and beans correct soil nitrogen levels to be perfect for corn. These techniques turned out to be a metaphor for how the garden grew, reflecting that all things work together, hopefully for the better.

The church developed a gardening ministry, which was mostly populated by elder women like Mama Maxine. Only one man, another elder, regularly showed up to help with the garden. Everyone else was in and out sporadically. Mama Maxine did not mince words when talking to Heber about her disappointment over the gendered division of labor. "I don't know why we can't get more men in this congregation to work in this garden," she told him. As much as farming is imagined to be "men's work," the women were the ones doing upkeep. Mama Maxine would show up to the garden early in the morning and come back late at night, and if the garden needed watering in between, you could count on her to do that too. No wonder she was fussing about getting more people, and men in particular, to do the work. Outside of Mama Maxine, the only person who spent more time in the garden was Heber. Though they struggled to get into a rhythm with volunteers from the church, there was plenty of interest outside of it. As Heber's message about the connections between food, faith, and farming gained popularity, more community members wanted to take part in the work he was leading. On weekends, students from nearby universities like Morgan State, Loyola, and Towson came to help. Whoever wanted to work the garden—community members, church members, students, out-of-towners—was welcome to do so. It was part of Heber's broader vision of building community, which was not exclusive to members of his church.

Once the garden began to produce, there was another question: what would they do with the harvest? Mama Maxine to the rescue again. Heber told me about her canning, another skill that she passed on to him. After harvest, she would take produce from the garden and, by the following Sunday, she'd be back at church with mason jars to pass out. Once, Mama Maxine handed Heber a jar with a handwritten label bearing her name and "chow chow." "I never heard of nothing called chow chow before!" We both laughed and I poked fun at Heber, asking if the Baltimore native was a *real* Southerner. Chow chow consists of summer vegetables like cabbage, tomatoes, and peppers that have been chopped, pickled, and stored to use as a relish throughout the year. In the rural East Texas community where I grew up, chow chow was a kitchen fixture—no less present or significant than salt, pepper, or running water. It was *that* important. Adding chow chow to collard greens and pinto beans and everything between is the casual country equivalent of what chefs might call *elevating* a dish. Chicagoans have giardiniera, a spicier version consisting of pickled peppers, carrots, celery, and cauliflower marinated in oil and spices. Haitians have piklinz, a spicy cabbage pickled in vinegar. Southerners, especially Black Southerners, have chow chow. Ranging from sweet to spicy, chow chow is the epitome of minimizing waste and maximizing sustainability—something that can carry you through colder, potentially harsher times of the year. Once again, Mama Maxine lived out the maxim of thrifty people across time and space: do a lot with a little.

They also gave away the fresh produce. Volunteers would set up a table near the church door on Sundays to allow congregants to take what they needed or wanted. This model created opportunities for buy-in. For the vision to work, congregants needed to understand the power of what was possible with the garden. Because most of the garden's activity happened during the church's off hours, sharing produce was not only a way to provide for the congregation, it also literally showed the fruit of the gardeners' labor.

After a while, the gardeners experimented with other approaches to see if the garden could support itself financially. They began asking for donations and then eventually moved to a fixed-price system. Heber would scout out the grocery stores in the area and then set lower prices for the garden's produce. Even though the church was selling its produce at an affordable price, there was still a concern about alienating people who needed food but couldn't pay. In Heber's mind, the solution to that was simple: those who could afford to pay, did; those who could not took whatever they needed free of charge. Unlike government programs like the Supplemental Nutritional Assistance Program (SNAP) or the Women, Infant, and Children (WIP) programs, there were no forms to fill out and no questions asked.

Setting prices was relatively easy. Getting people to spend their money on the church's produce rather than at the grocery store was more challenging. Most Americans are used to the convenience of getting everything they need from one place—a phenomenon that has its roots in improved home refrigeration, wide supermarket selection, and the ease of shopping day or night at a corporate store. Heber knew he couldn't compete with supermarkets on selection or hours. His strategy was to highlight the ways the church's garden provided a different kind of nourishment for the congregation and the community. For example, Pleasant Hope offered people an invitation to reflect and grow their capacity to give (and receive) according to their own measure.

Heber and his congregation didn't simply cultivate a garden at Pleasant Hope. They recognized and used an underappreciated church asset—land—in pursuit of something more amorphous: justice. One of the biggest lessons that gardens teach us is that assets exist everywhere, including in communities identified as having problems. Before you can leverage those assets, however, you first have to recognize them, as Mama Maxine and Heber did.

But assets alone do not create meaningful change. People do. Heber's deliberate process for organizing his community teaches us another lesson: for anything to be sustainable, we have to move only as quickly as a community's trust develops. For nearly two years, Heber moved his congregation toward feeling more comfortable with the idea of growing food in defiance of white supremacy. As a result, the church built an ecosystem around growing and distributing food. The work was a beautiful investment in their community. Little did Heber or Pleasant Hope know, it was only the beginning.

In April 2015, twenty-five-year-old Freddie Gray was arrested and sustained fatal injuries while in the custody of the Baltimore Police Department. Seven days after his arrest for possession of a knife, Gray died as the result of a severe spinal cord injury. His death was ruled a homicide.

Gray's death sparked protests and uprisings in Baltimore and beyond. For weeks, demonstrators gathered to protest racialized police brutality. The Baltimore police had long been criticized for their lack of transparency and excessive force. After the police refused to release details about the Gray investigation, tensions boiled over. Hours after his funeral on April 27, police and protesters clashed. Photos of that day show police in full riot gear rolling through the Baltimore streets in Humvees, and protesters attempting to protect their bodies from beatings and tear gas. The governor declared a state of emergency, and by dawn the next day additional police and the National Guard had been deployed. In a video addressed to the nation, President Obama said, "There is no excuse for the kind of violence that we saw yesterday. It is counterproductive. When individuals get crowbars and start prying open doors to loot, they're not protesting. They're not making a statement. They're stealing. When they burn down a building, they're committing arson. And they are destroying and undermining business and opportunities in their own communities."

Despite President Obama's admonition, people rebelled and were met with more violence. "A riot," Dr. Martin Luther King Jr. once said, "is the language of the unheard." And many in Baltimore felt their voices weren't being heard, so they shouted louder. Local businesses boarded up their windows. Grocery stores modified their hours, limited the number of people who could enter, or closed completely. Schools—often the only source of daily meals for the 84 percent of Baltimore students who received free or reduced-price lunch—closed. Following condemnation of Gray's death, the *New York Times* published an article that connected a rise in crime and a decrease in police presence in West Baltimore to activism demanding transparency and accountability. Police officers, Richard Oppel wrote, were reluctant to patrol neighborhoods like the one where Gray was arrested—not because of the crime rate, but because they feared public scrutiny of their actions. In an ostensible effort to connect increasing crime rates to a declining police presence due to community activism, Oppel sidestepped one of the primary criticisms of the Baltimore Police Department and others across the country: lack of accountability.

Heber resisted narratives that provided easy answers for who was at fault in the aftermath of Gray's death. He prioritized people—and some were hungry. He turned Pleasant Hope into a distribution center. People living in neighborhoods and towns all along the I-95 corridor delivered food to the church, and volunteers gave it away to anyone seeking assistance. "When city services backed up off the Black community," Heber said, "I saw an opportunity for the church to lean in." This moment—amid violence and the language of the unheard—birthed a national movement: the Black Church Food Security Network (BCFSN).

Heber recognized that there are Mama Maxines everywhere. When he had the idea to start a network of churches and farmers, it wasn't because he thought he or Pleasant Hope were special. Rather, it was because he felt they were so *ordinary*, an example of what the Black church could do anywhere and everywhere Black people gather—churched or unchurched. Other congregations have the same ingredients that Pleasant Hope had: land, a mandate to serve, and church mothers like Mama Maxine. He told me, "The profile of Mama Maxine is one that you can find in every church, so, yeah. She helped spark this idea that 'Wait, if there's nothing so special about Heber Brown or Pleasant Hope, then other churches can do it. Let's all do it.'"

I never met Mama Maxine in person—she passed away in 2018—but hearing Heber talk about her, I feel as if I knew her. She reminds me of many Black church mothers I know, extremely active in the church and community, highly skilled, and very protective of their pastors (when they love them). She sounded like my own Mama, my grandmother who gardened as many days as she could, fussed about church leadership, and moved mountains and molehills with the strength of her prayers and skills.

When Heber founded the BCFSN in 2015, he dreamed of creating a national alliance. The goal of many community gardens across the country is to address food insecurity and create opportunities for connection. Heber's vision was to create a whole ecosystem based on this shared mission, in which churches supported Black farmers, communities, and one another. The key to nourishment, according to him, is cooperation and co-creation. The mission is simple: to help Black churches use the assets they have to start gardens, host farmers markets, and buy from Black farmers with the goal of healing congregations, cities, and—in his wildest dreams—a nation.

Heber's vision is rooted in the reality that Black churches are some of the most stable landowners in Black communities. When Black people rebuilt their lives and communities after Emancipation, churches were among the first institutions established. And though polls show that younger people are less religious and attend church less often than their elders, Black churches remain important institutions. In rapidly gentrifying cities like Washington, D.C., and Oakland, California, for example, Black churches have built housing units on their property to respond to a growing affordable housing crisis. BCFSN seeks to do something similar with food.

What began as a response to the dire needs of Baltimoreans during the uprisings after Freddie Gray's murder grew into a movement within a familiar tradition. In the face of corporate and state neglect, we imagine otherwise. At this writing, over 250 churches in twenty-nine states have joined BCFSN. Together, congregations start new gardens and develop small farmers markets that feature Black farmers and operate on church property.

The early experiments with selling produce from Pleasant Hope's garden led to the development of the Soil to Sanctuary Market, or, as Heber described it, a farmers market inside a church. The market featured value-added products—like the chow chow Mama Maxine made—alongside produce from Black farmers across the region. There were also T-shirts, jewelry, and other handmade products from Black-owned businesses and, on some Sundays, cooking demonstrations by local chefs.

In some ways, the Soil to Sanctuary Market integrated everything Heber had learned about leading a church community toward life-affirming ministries, particularly those that appear different from more common charity-based approaches. Early in his work, he learned that people were afraid of what calling out white supremacy could mean for their church. Heber listened. What if calling out wasn't the focus. What if *calling in* was? The Soil to Sanctuary Market was an invitation: an invitation to congregants to connect directly with Black farmers, an invitation to artisans and cooks to proudly sell their products within an environment where the value of Blackness was not questioned but was instead the center of everything. And an invitation that mimicked what his idols Vernon Johns, Fannie Lou Hamer, and John the Baptist offered through their own ministries: that every person who attended would nourish themselves not only with food but also with the knowledge that these culturally relevant and affirming spaces were created with them in mind. With this market, Heber Brown redefined the wilderness as a place of feast and not famine.

Gardens are gathering places that grow our imaginations, our communities, and our capacity for self-determination. Pleasant Hope's asset-based approach was built on the expertise, skills, and culture that already existed within its congregation. Not only did Pleasant Hope's garden offer a way to increase food access, it also—perhaps more importantly—facilitated large- and small-scale transformations. Small gardens like Pleasant Hope's become the place where people learn skills, cultivate new relationships with the land and with others, and learn to see food as not only something to be consumed but as a catalyst for connection. Those transformations are part of the meaning of gathering. What Pleasant Hope was able to do with its garden, and what Heber later did to build an entire movement of Black churches, form a useful case study for how asset-based thinking can grow a small initiative into a national movement.

We can miss the point of gardens if we focus only on scaling up or on how many people can be fed. If Heber had eschewed the possibility of a 1,500-square-foot garden at Pleasant Hope Baptist Church, it is quite possible that there would have been no mutual aid efforts in the wake of Gray's murder and unlikely that BCFSN would have been founded either. Mama Maxine's insistence that you can do a lot with a little is revolutionary, perhaps even magical. Black people shouldn't have to do a lot with a little, but when we do, it increases one-hundred-fold—a modern-day example of Jesus feeding five thousand people with five loaves of bread and two fish. Every day, Black people like Heber and Mama Maxine take meager offerings, bless them, crack them open, and feed multitudes. Black studies theorist Saidiya Hartman might call gardens like Pleasant Hope's a part of making a wayward life, the kind of life that recognizes that it is pressed in on all sides by deadly, unjust systems but dares to breathe into the dream of freedom anyway. Wayward lives, insisting on freedom, with their commitment to nourishing community and bodies, are made and remade in spaces where the intention is clear: "Sit. Feast on your life." Your being is welcome here. When I consider the many ways in which improvisation has become part of the choreography of Black life in the Americas, these gardens come to mind as one setting in which they are practiced and perfected.

The example of Pleasant Hope Baptist Church shows us how the work of gathering is a slow, steady practice of putting one foot in front of the other. Heber gathered himself and then his church. He adapted his leadership style to *be with* the congregation he was leading and not just be ahead of them. It wasn't that they weren't open to change—they eventually embraced it—but they weren't ready for it. If we're not careful, we can easily mistake unreadiness as noncompliant, stubborn, or uninterested. Through listening, slowing down, and collaboration, Heber prepared his congregants. By doing so, he acknowledged the gap between what was and what could be, while honoring the agency of the people he aimed to move forward.

As the church meeting early in his tenure demonstrated, congregants expected him to earn their trust and support. They weren't unlike many people across the country, who may be skeptical or at least reticent about food justice initiatives in their neighborhoods. One lesson we might take from Heber and Pleasant Hope is that most folks aren't looking toward food justice as an antidote if it means taking away their autonomy or their voices. To create sustainable change, leaders must be willing to surrender their plans to the necessary, sometimes painfully long process of relationship-building. I loved listening to Heber talk about Mama Maxine. His stories about her demonstrated a truth that many of us can learn from: every single one of us needs someone to vouch for us and our vision for a better food world. And every single one of us needs someone to mentor us in bringing those visions to fruition. Even leaders. Perhaps especially leaders.

After thirteen years as pastor of Pleasant Hope Baptist Church, Heber stepped down in 2022. Initially, he continued to work the garden, wanting to see it thrive. But he reluctantly gave that up too, as he worried his presence at the church would overshadow the next pastor. Still, Heber's legacy will live on; he transformed a congregation and birthed a movement. With his vision, his careful approach to leading people who were skeptical, and his commitment to creating something that validates the goodness of the people he wanted to serve, Heber gave us more than a how-to for growing gardens. He gave us a blueprint for growing connections and community.

CHAPTER 2

REUNIONS

—

To get to the Johnson family reunion, I drove from my visit with Heber Brown in Baltimore to Delmar, Delaware. It was an uneventful trip, two hours over bridges and through fields and fields of agricultural production, yet there was something awe-inspiring and calming about that drive. I thought about how often these agricultural fields get left out of narratives about the Northeast. The South and the Midwest get characterized as where things are grown, and the Northeast is where things are . . . thought about? But I had already seen all the ways that these categories were proven false. Cities like Baltimore can host gardens and farms with the potential to transform the city, and even places that seem initially uninterested in food justice can offer fertile ground for social movements to flourish. Food justice could grow just about anywhere.

It was a perfect day for a reunion: not a cloud in the sky, not too hot, and, importantly, the air was clear. The week prior, smoke from Canadian wildfires had traveled south, cloaking the eastern corridor of the US in a health-threatening smog. When I was in Baltimore, the air smelled like plastic through my five-ply mask, and the atmosphere was hazy. Philadelphia was experiencing the worst air quality in the world at the time, and since it is only 130 miles north of Delmar, I worried that the family reunion would be canceled, but on that morning the smoke had lifted considerably. The sun looked normal and not an angry red.

When I announced through social media that I was looking to attend Black family reunions as part of my research on food justice, Crystal was among the first to respond. We've known each other for over twenty years. When she was an undergraduate student at Baylor University in Waco, Texas, she attended the church my godfather pastored, and over time, he and my godmother treated her as one of their own. When I was an undergraduate at Trinity University in San Antonio a few years later, her parents did the same for me. The invitation to join her and her family, the Johnsons, at the reunion was a welcome one. I had not seen Crystal in almost ten years, and it had been much longer since I'd seen her parents. Social media keeps you up-to-date on people's lives, but there is no substitute for gathering.

Earlier that morning, I texted Crystal, "Good morning! It's a beautiful day for a family reunion!!!" She let me know that she and her family were also en route. She was clearly excited but also nervous about how everything would go. One of her aunts who lived in the area oversaw planning the food, and Crystal was worried about it, ending her last text to me with "we hope everyone can eat . . . hahaha." In every Black family, there is someone, often multiple someones, worried that there won't be enough food.

The Johnson reunion was small, and it had come together quickly, after only a few months of planning. They opted to gather in a public park in Delmar—about twenty minutes from Salisbury, Maryland, where Crystal's mom, Annette, and her siblings had grown up. It was also where Aunt Helen still lived. With many of the family members coming from out of town or out of state, including Crystal and her parents, it was useful for the reunion to be near someone who could take care of any local needs. When I arrived at the park around 12:30 p.m., the Johnsons were setting up portable tables and chairs. As the adults handled setup, the children played on the playground with two family dogs or on the basketball courts. Though this wasn't the dirt road and open fields that I grew up with, watching kids run around with few restrictions reminded me that freedom is a fundamental experience at family reunions—if for no other reason, trust is an underlying value. Safe spaces aren't a given; they are created. With the right people and the right intentions, they can be created almost anywhere.

"Welcome to the Johnson Family Reunion 2023!" Mrs. Annette shouted. We all clapped in response. "We've got our patriarch here. We've got four out of our five siblings. [At] all our previous reunions, we always had Aunt Somebody, Uncle Somebody, an older cousin, but now we're the older ones. Some of you I haven't seen in years and years and years. We're going to mingle. We're going to bless this food. After we bless the food, we're gonna have our first drawing of the day. It's nothing much. It's just little gifts. So, if you hear me holler, come around for the drawings, okay? Anybody have anything to say before we bless the food?" Mrs. Annette's grandson offered the prayer, thanking God for the food we'd receive, and with that, the Johnson family reunion was officially underway.

Mrs. Annette pointed people toward hand sanitizer and plates and told them where to line up for the buffet. Crystal, her sister, and I lined up behind the food tables, armed ourselves with gloves and serving utensils, and got to work. Together, we uncovered pans of baked chicken, pulled pork, grilled hot dogs and burgers, green beans, potato salad, baked beans, and macaroni salad. On a separate table, we stacked piles of hot dog and hamburger buns alongside homemade cookies and other desserts. With so many people traveling from out of town, the family opted to have the food catered by a local Black woman chef. The caterer hung around, making sure the food was up to everyone's standards. When she was sure everything was all good, she left. As we continued to set up, Aunt Helen slid one red bowl with homemade collard greens alongside the aluminum foil containers. She might have been okay with having the food catered, but she was not giving up the responsibility of making greens! When I tasted them, I understood why. Later, the look of satisfaction on Aunt Helen's face as she collected the empty red bowl was confirmation that her greens had made the statement she intended for them to make.

If Crystal's mother was in charge, then Crystal was a matriarch in training. Just as commanding—if not as loud—as her mom, Crystal always had a penchant for order. A former ROTC cadet who was commissioned into the Air Force after college, Crystal had spent twenty years and counting in the military making order out of chaos. Before the reunion started, she made sure the elders were taken care of, looked after the little ones, and didn't hesitate to offer structure during a chaotic moment. After the extra chairs were set up and the food had been delivered, Crystal sent someone to gather the children while she spoke to each elder to let them know what they should expect. As the food was being served and the reunion was well underway, Mrs. Annette turned to Crystal to figure out when to start drawing names for the raffle prizes.

That the reunion was organized by the women in the family was not out of the ordinary. With few exceptions, women took on a significant portion of the labor for the reunions I attended and the ones interviewees shared memories about. Women, Black women, in particular, are often the glue that holds families together. They're the genealogists and archivists, the caretakers and the cooks. They're often doing more labor than they should—one of the ways we can see how patriarchy shows up everywhere, even in how we gather.

People lined up to be served. Kiddos were first, mostly opting for a hamburger or hot dog. Sometimes they'd ask for two, and I'd tell them that if they ate the first, they could come back for seconds—the kind of gentle, loving correction that is allowed and expected in safe spaces. This is my preferred way to be at gatherings. I love to serve, and it is a way that I can be involved without having to make a whole lot of small talk.

Before the first raffle Mrs. Annette asked her brother to introduce himself. "My name is Frank Johnson, and evidently I'm now the patriarch of the family, which means I'm the oldest," he started. Pop Frankie, as he was called, continued with a rundown of the family tree: "My father was Frank Johnson, also called the cake man. My mother was Daisy Johnson. My grandmother was Ella Peters. And I had several aunts. I belong to all of them." Crystal's mother, Pop Frankie's sister, lovingly interrupted him, knowing that if you let him, he'd talk all day. After the raffle, I approached Pop Frankie and introduced myself. I told him I was a friend of Crystal's, but I was also an anthropologist. We worked our way through a familiar-to-me conversation. He asked if anthropology was like digging for bones. I said that kind of work is connected to anthropology but not exactly the same. "It's more like I dig for people's stories about their communities and cultures," I said. He seemed satisfied with that explanation. "Since you're the patriarch, I imagine you have a lot of memories about your family reunions," I said encouragingly.

Pop Frankie started at the beginning. He painted a scene of racially segregated Washington, D.C., and the adjacent Maryland suburbs in the 1940s and 1950s:

> Back in the '40s, the late '40s, after World War II and going into the Korean War, Black children still were in Black schools. It wasn't until 1955 that we really integrated. I can remember taking my chair when I was in the third grade from one school, Wilson Elementary School, and going from there to a white school in Washington, D.C. [Black communities] used to have gardens and stuff in the back where they would grow beets. Now, most Black families in Washington, D.C., had a garden in the back. Yes, they had a garden in the back, and they had fresh vegetables because they migrated from the South. Almost every household had a chicken, or a couple chickens where they'd get their eggs and everything. Thompson Milk Company was allowed to deliver milk to the Black community. That's how we got our milk. Every Friday, the fish man came back. That's when we got our fish and everything.

For Pop Frankie, this was more than historical context. His experiences growing up in Washington and living through the transition to federally mandated integration informed his understanding of what separateness meant. To some extent, Pop Frankie's early life was shaped as much by what he couldn't do as by what he could. He couldn't ride in the front of streetcars because he was Black. He couldn't go to certain parks without risking arrest. He couldn't go to the big movie theaters downtown. But these constraints cemented the significance of what it meant to create conditions where Black people could gather and thrive. For him, that togetherness was intimately bound to food.

Without any prompting from me, Pop Frankie illustrated the ways that food production, distribution, and procurement were community-based practices that thrived during his childhood despite racial segregation. This is a sentiment I'd heard from other elders many times before. As one of my research participants from earlier research in Washington, D.C., put it, after integration, "Black folks started looking at some of the things like farming and they looked at that as associated with that feeling of 'Oh, we're not slaves.' I guess folks became too sophisticated to dig in the ground." For both Pop Frankie and my previous research participant, there was a connection between changes in the social fabric of the country and the weakening of family ties and gatherings. While neither man would suggest that racism was beneficial to Black people, they emphasized that shared struggle forged bonds and practices that created strong communities. In the same way, family reunions are opportunities for people to cultivate and maintain meaningful connections with one another.

Despite Crystal's fears, there was plenty of food left as the reunion started to wind down. Some people loaded to-go plates, but most of the leftovers were carefully packed up to be donated to a Christian-based outreach center and homeless shelter, an arrangement made by Aunt Helen prior to the reunion's start. When I arrived at the shelter to drop off the food, people were mingling outside while the volunteer cooks and servers assembled in the kitchen for prayer. They waved me in and made space for me in the circle, and we all bowed our heads and gave thanks for the meals that would be shared.

On the drive back to Baltimore, I reflected on Aunt Helen's forethought about leftovers. Thinking about and planning for what happens *after* consumption is not often a priority. Americans throw away about 133 billion pounds of food every year, an estimated 30–40 percent of the food supply. Nearly 52 percent of this waste comes from the food industry itself. Grocery stores in particular discard "ugly" fruits and vegetables, foods that are near their expiration dates, and foods that are damaged during transport, if they don't choose to redistribute them. Organizations like Food Recovery Network, a national student-led organization, collect surplus food from across the food chain and donate it to people who are food-insecure. Their work is another example of ordinary people addressing a social problem by marshaling their assets and strengths. Despite waste being primarily a food industry–created problem, the Food Recovery Network sees it as a shared responsibility to address it with the aim of transforming waste into security for others.

In her decades-long career researching poverty and hunger, sociologist Jan Poppendieck offered two distinct ways that food insecurity has been addressed in the US: via a charity model and a justice model. The charity model, she explained, emphasizes "voluntarism, neighborliness, localism, spiritual good, and personal involvement," while a justice model emphasizes "dignity, entitlement, accountability, and equity." For Poppendieck, the justice model is predicated on mutuality—treating food insecurity as an issue that impacts everyone and one which we all have some responsibility in addressing. Food justice organizations like the National Black Food and Justice Alliance (NBFJA) push this idea further by arguing that any vision of justice also needs to shift ownership in our food system such that those who have been most impacted by its harms have some control over its future—from how and where food is grown to creating distribution models that center equity and ultimately to what is actually consumed. Justice models require radical shifts in the food system that require time, labor, money, and, most importantly, redistribution of power. It's one reason why the charity model has become the basis of how food insecurity is managed in the US. Food banks, food pantries, Meals on Wheels, etc.—collectively known as emergency food provisioning—have grown in number and size since the 1980s. In 2023, more than 50 million people received charitable food assistance at least once.

This number is extraordinary and points to several intersecting challenges that impact people's ability to feed themselves and their families. Stagnant wages mean that incomes are not keeping up with the price of groceries; uneven distribution of grocery stores means that groceries are not accessible or convenient for everyone; and US food aid policies have not provided enough of a safety net to make sure everyone's basic nutritional needs are met. In the absence of living wages, adequate access, and progressive policies, emergency food provisioning has been an important mechanism that can be the difference between some people having a meal to eat and going hungry. Poppendieck's distinction between charity and justice isn't about demonizing emergency food provisioning. Instead, she draws the distinction as a cautionary tale. The more emergency food provisioning becomes the standard in place of a social safety net that should be provided by the government, the more we undermine the philosophy that food itself is a human right, not a gift that is dependent on someone else's charitable heart.

So, how should we understand Aunt Helen's planning in the context of food waste, charity, and justice? Quite simply, this is the same kind of care that the emergency food provisioning system relies on. We all know an Aunt Helen or have been her. Who do you know who has prepared hot meals for Meals on Wheels? How many times have you volunteered to sort donations at your local food bank, scanning expiration dates, separating cans, or preparing boxes to be picked up by or delivered to families in need? Perhaps you have been on the receiving end of such acts—waiting in line at church pantries, sitting down at local organizations that serve hot meals, or quite simply hoping a neighbor or friend will bless you with enough of their own abundance to get by. This kind of charity-based giving-and-receiving is familiar to most of us and is so much less daunting than a justice approach, which requires us to change so much about how we understand food. That is why emergency food provisioning feels so accessible, tangible, and familiar. It is made up of everyday people like you and me. Aunt Helen's plan to donate leftovers from the reunion connected her to thousands of people who choose to serve others rather than produce more waste.

FAMILY REUNIONS AREN'T OBVIOUS case studies for food justice. In fact, there is tension between a typical reunion menu and some of the core tenets that drive food justice movements. Often taking the form of a large cookout, barbecue, or fish fry, Black family reunion meals are filled with foods that we're constantly warned will lead to obesity, diabetes, hypertension, and other diet-related illnesses. Hamburgers, hot dogs, chips, sodas, Kool-Aid, and more are readily available, and most people, especially children, grab them with little thought.

Perhaps more than any other group, Black people's consumption is heavily policed and stigmatized. Because of racism and stigma, Black people's food consumption doesn't get contextualized. Take, for example, the way that soul food is derided and cited as a reason for health-related conditions, even though those large meals are often only served on special occasions or at Sunday dinners. From a public health or food justice standpoint, framing Black food traditions as harmful is more of the norm and less of an exception. At every turn, the foods that Black people eat are taken as examples of lack, unhealthiness, or excess. Pathologizing Black people and what they eat puts us further away from food justice, not closer. Creating stark binaries between "healthy" and "unhealthy" misses a core element of food justice itself—that it isn't about forcing people to eat a certain way. Even as we advocate for increasing awareness and access, we can do so in a manner that honors community and maintains the conditions for nourishment.

Though the menus at reunions vary, it isn't necessarily the food itself that carries the most significance. It is the whole *vibe*: that sense of belonging, safety, and care. Geographer Kaily Heitz has emphasized that the vibe of Black gatherings and spaces can be felt in the promise of offering safety in the ever-present threat of racialized violence—even if it is temporary. The vibe is the feeling of being held.

Food is an integral part of creating this vibe. American studies professor Psyche Williams-Forson has called this "Black food energy." It's difficult to define, but you know it when you hear it, smell it, *feel it*. She wrote, "Black food energy can be hard to explain, but one may know it when they experience it. It is why the combination of macaroni and cheese, collard greens, and fried chicken is familiar to many Black people, though these are arguably not 'Black foods.'" It is the foods themselves, and their smells commingled with other familiar scents like shea butter, coupled with the sounds of Maze and Frankie Beverly's "Before I Let Go" and free-roaming children, that create an atmosphere that matters for how we understand nourishment. Vibe matters—if for no other reason than that the atmosphere of a gathering or a place lets people know whether they're welcome. It's the history, meaning, and energy behind the gatherings themselves. The intentions behind these gatherings can serve as inspiration for food justice movements that face challenges with balancing bureaucracy and measuring their impact with building an inclusive, holistic movement that inspires people.

I witnessed the impacts and possibilities of these gatherings firsthand when I visited Parks, Louisiana. Convening for the first time in over twenty years, the Ebow family reunion gathered over two hundred people for a three-day celebration in the shadows of sugarcane and the St. John Plantation. Chassidy, the friend who invited me, was impressed with the size of the gathering. "You usually only get this kind of turnout with a funeral," she commented.

The Ebow family created an altar in honor of family members who had passed. The altar included unlit red candles, a trifold board with photos and names of ancestors who represented different parts of the family tree, and a framed copy of the marriage certificate of the family's matriarch and patriarch from January 1900. They also organized a family-history tour of the town led by elders. The oldest members of the family boarded an air-conditioned van to lead the way. The rest of us filed into cars and lined up to follow them, dialing into a conference call that linked us to the elders. While we drove from one place to another, we listened to elders take turns sharing stories and histories about various places. "Can y'all hear me now?" an elder asked over the microphone. We actually couldn't hear her well. The van, carrying about ten elders over sixty-five, was abuzz with chatter and crosstalk that made it difficult for the rest of us to catch whole sentences. Chassidy and I joked that a bus full of elders who weren't familiar with technology was a recipe for adventure. Despite the tech mishaps, we tried to grasp all the wisdom they were sharing. Every stop was a place that was significant to their ancestral legacy: the matriarch's former home, the big house on the plantation where the family was enslaved, and the cemetery where their loved ones were buried. When we got to the cemetery, we went in search of Mama Tune's, the matriarch's, grave.

I followed the crowd and listened to snatches of conversation. One of the elders led us down one row and then another in search of the grave, sometimes getting sidetracked by pointing out other headstones. When it became clear that we weren't on a direct path to Mama Tune, people wandered in different directions until someone shouted, "We found it!" A couple of people lovingly brushed leaves from the aboveground grave, and there was an unplanned moment of silence in reverence to their ancestor. After, some members of the family lamented about how neglected her tomb looked compared to others. It was a shame that they didn't have someone come out and tend to her grave on a regular basis, someone said. Another offered that if even half of the people who were attending the reunion would give twenty-five dollars a year, they could more than afford to pay someone to be a caretaker. What was designed to be a trip down family history lane turned out to be an opportunity for the family to reflect on how to be better stewards of their family's legacy, including

Mama Tune's grave. This also reminds us that the only way any long-term care is sustainable is if it is collective.

The reverence and remembrance practiced at the Ebow reunion were important factors in other reunions as well, though each family practiced them differently. The Cockrill family held their reunion right outside Nashville, Tennessee, near where their family is from. I was invited by Travonnie, someone I knew from teaching middle school in Atlanta, and I was excited to attend because it was the first reunion they'd had since the Covid-19 pandemic. After a four-year hiatus, the Cockrills were resuming a ritual they'd begun in 1987. Hearing this, I was overcome by the reality that all rituals can be broken or interrupted. I believe that rituals are the lifeblood of almost everything—from how and where we eat, to how we honor those who've passed on, to how we celebrate life. Anthropologists have long been interested in rituals, precisely because they are key practices that keep people connected to one another.

The Saturday portion of the Cockrill reunion began at noon, to give people an hour to settle in before the official start, which was the family headcount and prayer. They convened at a pavilion with eight tables for people to sit at and about half as many for serving food, plus five or so portable tents where people huddled to stay out of the sun. Most attendees, however, were spread out in pockets, sitting casually in camp chairs with the people they knew most intimately, moving around to catch snatches of shade cast by the surrounding trees.

When one o'clock rolled around, L.A.Monz, one of the members of the reunion committee and the apparent go-to person for questions and directions, corralled everyone into an open space with a single tree. He moved around the various crowds effortlessly, and it was clear that most people there knew and respected him. He was warm but also dutiful, making sure to hug and greet people while also moving them in the right direction so that the reunion could formally start. L.A.Monz was one of few men I witnessed in a visible leadership position at a family reunion. Later, I would meet Rasheed, L.A.Monz's cousin, who is also on the committee. When I told them it stood out to me to have men in leadership in this way, both paused to consider it before Rasheed responded, "Well, it's what we saw. Granddaddy, some of our uncles, all the old-school guys. [The reunion] was a time for them." After another brief pause, he added, "I mean, you find that unusual, but I think it's sad." Both L.A.Monz and Rasheed wondered if this was a sign of the times. They reminisced about old times when they weren't *asked* to be involved but were *told*—a stark contrast in philosophies around not only parenting but how to convey responsibility to kids. They both admitted that they worried what would become of the reunion if anything happened to them.

Those worries weren't at the forefront on reunion day, though. As L.A.Monz put us in place for the family count, there was bubbling excitement in the air. We formed two circles: one of children who circled the tree, and a wider one of adults encompassing them. The family elders gathered under a nearby pavilion to stay out of the heat while the reunion committee got everyone in order. Once the circles were mostly formed, the DJ began playing the unofficial Black American family reunion theme song—the O'Jays' 1975 classic "Family Reunion," from the album of the same name. "It's a family reunion, y'all!" someone yelled over the microphone, and everyone erupted in cheers as the instrumental introduction gave way to the lyrics.

Under the pavilion, the elders swayed and held hands. As a few of them sang along to the O'Jays, they met one another's gaze, squeezing hands for emphasis. Sunrays picked up hints of tears, making me wonder what it felt like to be the remaining elders with fewer years ahead than behind them, whose responsibility included sharing family history and stories. Seeing the family gather again in this way after a lengthy hiatus meant something to the elders. Family reunions are rituals that are in part about memory and remembrance, yes. But for some elders, they are also about marveling that the universe kept them alive long enough to see the fruits of their labor: three or four living generations, including dozens of children who, hopefully, would carry on this ritual for years to come. A year after the reunion, I sent Travonnie a text with a clip of the elders holding hands and singing with the note, "Revisiting photos and videos from your reunion, and this one made me teary-eyed! You can just tell that being able to gather in this way after the covid years meant everything to them." She quickly replied: "Oh absolutely!!! We lost [two] of those elders this year. This is such precious footage." Hearing about their loss triggered both sadness and gratitude in me: sadness about their deaths and gratitude that, as an anthropologist who was invited into their space, I had had the privilege of capturing this tender moment. I asked Travonnie their names and knew then that I'd honor them in some way in the pages of this book. Ms. Josephine Searcy and Mr. James Buntin, we speak your names.

When the song ended, L.A.Monz stepped to the mic to set the intention for the weekend:

We've lost many of our loved ones from Covid, to other sickness, to gun violence, and so today we are here standing together united as a family. And this is what it is all about and shall be about. And the reason we have the young folks in the center is so they can watch and look out at us older folks and learn and have these memories and take them on so that when we're long gone, they will continue to have a reunion and carry this thing on. All right?

He announced that that morning a family member had passed away and another was on life support. His urging to take these moments together as a gift reminded me of a quote from geographer Ruth Wilson Gilmore: "Where life is precious, life is precious," meaning that when we start from the premise that every life is valuable, our institutions and rituals are molded to reflect that belief. At reunions like this one, people who have been out of touch or far away come back into the fold, even if they've been gone for a long time. Strangers—like me—are assumed to be family. Among the Cockrills, I was hugged no less than ten times, even before I'd been introduced. In that space, my life was precious, and they reminded me of that.

After L.A.Monz's words, we transitioned to the counting. This ritual started with the first Cockrill reunion in 1987. Grainy footage of those early days showed loved ones who had long passed on, Travonnie as an adorable toddler, and a younger version of the family's oldest member, Ms. Josie. The family count started with her. At eighty-six years old, she had bested the average life expectancy for Black people by fifteen years. Ms. Josie started the count by declaring "one" in the mic. From there, the count moved through each elder, around the outer circle with the adults and then the children's circle in the middle. L.A.Monz held the mic up to each person—some shouted their number confidently, while some were timid, and a few were distracted and not sure about what number they were until those nearby chided them. The higher the number, the greater the anticipation. When the count reached one hundred, cheers rippled around the circle. But we weren't even halfway done. The count continued, and the excitement grew. As we got closer to the end, someone beside me whispered, "We're going to break two hundred!" After three minutes forty-five seconds, every family member who was present had been accounted for—all 208 of them. Travonnie's mom grabbed the microphone and prayed over the gathering:

> Inhabit this place and nourish us, God. Bless our elderly. We have to keep them lifted up. Remember who our elderly are today, God. We continue to pray and thank you for giving them to us so that we can cast a shadow for those [young people] that are standing in the middle circle so they will carry out your wishes. We ask these and all your blessings, God. In your darling son Jesus's name we pray. Amen.

The circles and the prayer that affirmed them were powerful. They represented unity and the cycle of life, starting with the eldest and ending with the youngest who would carry the torch forward. I filmed the count, bearing witness to how the circles served as a beautiful metaphor for this family's will to remain connected. Loss has a way of either bringing people together or severing connections. Given the losses the family had experienced, the Cockrill reunion was a powerful reminder that maintaining connection is a choice, even if it is arduous.

L.A.Monz, Rasheed, and the rest of the committee worked hard to make the reunion look effortless, but beneath the love was labor and a costly endeavor. Every year people asked if there would be a reunion, Rasheed reflected, but few volunteered to help without being nudged to do so. Most years, the reunion dues, holding steady for a while at sixty-five dollars per family unit and an additional twenty dollars per T-shirt, didn't cover the full cost of it. Yet no one was ever turned away—even if they didn't chip in, an unofficial rule that Rasheed and L.A.Monz laughingly disagreed on. Rasheed felt they should be stricter about collecting dues—not so much because of the money itself but as a reflection of collective responsibility. For L.A.Monz, it was important that they didn't get caught up on the finances. He believed that even if having a successful reunion meant contributing more money from his own pocket, seeing things like the family count and people reuniting was all worth it. There were so many details, but if you got lost in them, the beauty of the gathering got lost too. "You have to love it," L.A.Monz said. "You have to love it, and you have to put your feelings into it, or you won't do it."

The ritual reminded me of the Logans in Mildred D. Taylor's 1981 children's novel *Let the Circle Be Unbroken*. Taylor chronicled the struggles and joys of a Black sharecropping family in Mississippi. After their son and brother Stacey and his friend Moe ran away to find work in the sugarcane fields of Louisiana, the family found itself waking up on Christmas morning feeling incomplete. They gathered in a circle to sing "Will the Circle Be Unbroken?" as they did every Christmas morning, but with no word from Stacey and Moe, this year's Christmas ritual felt different. Each family member—holding love and loss—offered praise and prayers for safe returns to complete their circle. Taylor's fictional family mirrors real-life Black families

I had the pleasure of engaging with. Despite loss, despite disruption to family traditions, there is no question mark here. Where the song asks a question—will the circle be unbroken?—the title of Taylor's novel is much more fitting for the families I visited. "Let the circle be unbroken" is a prayer and a command—a speaking into existence that, after and amid loss, there will be celebration.

Black family reunions have a long history that dates to the early days of Emancipation. After gaining freedom, reuniting with lost family members was a priority for most African Americans. In *Help Me to Find My People*, historian Heather Williams chronicled the persistent, often heartbreaking efforts of those newly freed who put all their will and resources toward reconnecting with their families. She analyzed over 1,200 "Information Wanted" and "Lost Friends" advertisements that appeared in the 1860s and 1870s, many of which were placed in Black newspapers. It is likely that some of these advertisements were dictated to newspaper staff who were responsible for writing them, because many of the searchers would not have been able to read or write. I was curious if anyone from my hometown had placed advertisements like the ones Williams detailed. My breath caught in my throat when my search of Last Seen: Finding Family After Slavery, a digital archive of these information-wanted advertisements, yielded five results related to Crockett, Texas. On July 21, 1881, Matt Terry placed an ad in the *Southwestern Christian Advocate* in New Orleans, Louisiana. It read:

> DEAR EDITOR: I desire to inquire for my mother—Harriet Wood, who left me in Crockett, Texas, in 1861. Her name at first was Harriet Terry. She used to be hired by Mr. Thomas Croditt, in Crockett. She was the mother of four children—three girls

and one boy named as follows: Francis, Mittie, Maria, and Matt Terry. My father was Ned Calvin, but he is dead. My sisters and I are living here in Houston county, near Crockett, where she left us, and we are all members of the M. E. Church. There will be ten dollars given to any one who will find my mother. Address me at Crockett, Houston Co., Texas. MATT TERRY.

The other ads placed in search of people near my hometown were much the same: Mrs. Eliza Jones placed an ad in the *Houston Daily Post* on February 24, 1898, looking for her father's brother, Sam Roberson. Sam Grant's 1882 appeal in the *Southwestern Christian Advocate* appeared nearly thirty years after he was brought to Texas from Tennessee. He hadn't seen his sister since he was ten years old. Jiles Hunley wrote from Crockett in search of his unnamed mother, whom he had not seen in thirty years, his sister Martha Jane, and his wife's sons John and Madison, whom she'd last seen in Tennessee. These advertisements, filled with hope and longing, are some of the earliest examples of Black people following the impulse to be together, to gather.

Over 150 years later, I found myself hoping that these people were reunited with their families and felt sad knowing that, given the odds, it would have been a miracle if they had been. I could only imagine the feeling of placing an ad like this, how you'd want the whole world to stop so you could search for your people. This longing would be stacked against the reality that you had to push forward with living—with or without your lost loved one. I've tried to imagine the agony of disappointment, the cruel reality of overburdened charitable organizations and of failed government programs intended to reunify families torn apart by slavery. I imagined that no matter how many advertisements you placed, you would never feel like you'd done enough.

For many of those who submitted advertisements, the desire to gather—to hug those torn from them by violence and terror, to celebrate that white supremacy did not steal everything—was never fulfilled. Elements of that longing, hope, disappointment, and celebration that families had in the late 1800s linger today. No matter how difficult it was to organize, no matter the expense, no matter the level of participation, every person I talked to about their reunion traditions agreed that it was something that they wanted to hang on to. In some families, like the Johnsons and the Cockrills, family members worried that younger generations wouldn't pick up the mantle to keep the tradition going. Without fail, reunion organizers addressed this at their gatherings, imploring young people to see the value of coming together in person.

There are some experiences that just can't be replicated online, the kind of serendipitous moments that remind you of the value of sharing physical space together. Perhaps the most amazing part of the Cockrill reunion was the impromptu tug-o'-war with another family, who were having their very first family reunion in the same park. The Cockrills in their Kente-patterned T-shirts and the Davises in their powder-blue tees hyped themselves up to the beat of Mystikal's "Here I Go!" As the friendly rivalry between two families who'd just met got underway, the strongest attendees, mostly men, lined up to take the rope. The self-proclaimed referee turned to one family and then the other to ask, "Are you ready?" When both responded yes, he shouted: "On your mark! Get Set! PULL!" It took the Cockrills seven seconds to drag the Davises across the center line. The crowd erupted in cheers; shirts twirled around like spirit rags. The Davis family regrouped for round two. Despite their best efforts to dig their heels deep into the earth, they were dragged across the center line again. This time, the DJ blasted C-Murder's "Down 4 My N's." After their loss, the tug-o'-war arena transformed into a swag surf-turned-dance circle party as the DJ cycled between club classics and line dance songs. There was little distinction between the two groups other than their T-shirts—strangers-turned-kin, if only for the moment.

If there was one thing I experienced at all the reunions I attended, it was radical hospitality—the inclusion of people who weren't family members without question or contestation. Even though I was invited to each family reunion by only one person, having them vouch for me was enough. I was an outsider in the sense that I wasn't formally connected to each family, but I was kinfolk by choice. Radical hospitality means making room for others with whom we don't have an immediate connection. Imagine: What would food justice look and feel like if it was oriented around a practice like radical hospitality? It would require us to expand our definitions of kinship and of who belongs and who doesn't. Radical hospitality means setting a table, expecting that there will be guests you didn't plan for, and having extra seats just in case. I was offered one of those seats, and it meant everything to know that my presence wasn't a burden or a chore. I was a welcome addition.

I HAVE ATTENDED MORE family reunions than I can count. My family has an annual reunion that ninety-five-year-old Uncle Jim said started in the 1960s. The branches of our family tree are varied and many. My mother is one of seven, and her father, whose family landed in East Texas, was one of fourteen children. If we mapped the children and grandchildren of my grandfather and his siblings, the branches would span the state of Texas and well beyond. We were one of the branches who stayed on the inherited land, my mother opting to keep us close to our grandparents, our grandmother in particular, in Cooper Settlement, an unincorporated part of Houston County right outside of the small town of Crockett.

Growing up in Cooper Settlement meant that I gathered with my cousins regularly. Kim and Tiffani lived at opposite ends of the dirt road that served as a tether between us, and I was in the middle. We would meet along the road and play outside the whole day. As dusk settled over our insulated community, we'd follow my grandmother's instructions to walk each other a piece of the way home. Being able to do this—play with cousins openly in the streets and the woods, walk freely at dusk—undoubtedly structured my deep belief that I have a right to live without inhibition. This is a sort of mundanity I wish for all people.

When our annual family reunion drew nearer, there was always a different buzz in the community, one of anticipation. It meant that the dirt road I traveled every day had new sojourners, those far-flung aunties and cousins it carried back home. I cannot say how the city contingent of our family felt when they were in the city, but I would describe the feeling of their return to this homeplace in a simple term: relief.

The Johnson and Cockrill family reunions, though different in style and size, represent a beloved tradition that cultivates connection and care in the context of anti-Black violence—the all-encompassing weather that structures Black life. For many Black families—especially those who do not have a family home or land to return to or whose family is so large that it rotates from region to region, the reunion is not just an opportunity to reunite. It is also an opportunity to transform public space and create a haven. That these reunions often happen in public spaces is no small detail. Many families, like the Cockrills, choose to host their reunions in city parks. These are the same kind of public spaces where a twelve-year-old Black boy gets shot by police for playing with a toy, where BBQ Beckys call the police on Black people for gathering for cookouts, or where bird-watching while Black results in threats of violence. Hosting these events in public parks is a reclamation of public spaces that we all have a right to but that are not always safe or available to Black people. If public squares in the US have historically been places where Black people were bought, sold, dehumanized, and humiliated, then parks that host reunions become containers for reconciliation, healing, joy, and a form of quiet resistance that says we ain't going nowhere.

These outdoor places help facilitate Black self-recovery. Safety is cultivated there. Children run freely, and parents can feel confident that they will be protected. Political conversations happen here. Over plates of barbecue, people discuss the dire economic condition of their hometown or the country's future. Mourning happens here. At the reunions I attended, families called the names of people who had passed on in recent years, lit candles, and displayed photos of matriarchs and patriarchs. At these gatherings, no one is forgotten, even if some are only spoken of in whispers. Nonbiological kin become family, and strangers—like me—are vouched for and brought into the fold. Leadership grows there. Watching my friend Crystal, it was easy to see that if the Johnson family reunion tradition continues into the next decade, it will be because she made it so.

Pleasure is experienced there. Joy is cultivated there. Black family reunions are a whole vibe.

Reunions are perfect places to look for inspiration for a food justice movement that is redefining itself. Reunions create connection, provide opportunities to practice care, and are containers for cultivating a sense of safety—all factors that are important aspects of community and individual foodways. Freedom, joy, anticipation, and home-grown leadership coalesce in ways that may not be measurable but are impactful. Reunions have internal organization systems that center communalism, commensality—the shared activities around food—and connection, the less measurable aspects of living a well-nourished life. Sociologist and food studies scholar Alice P. Julier pointed to these less measurable aspects as important for understanding what commensality teaches us about social arrangements and inequality. To understand what society values, simply follow the food. Following the food doesn't only tell us about society as a whole. It also tells us about how ancestral connections and memory, the will to gather with kin, the satisfaction we derive from sharing a good meal, and the reclamation of public space coalesce to create nourishment for the entire being.

At a seminar about this work, I remarked that satisfaction is an underexplored concept in food justice but is something that we can witness, experience, and learn from at family reunions. Charity, emergency food provisioning, or simply providing the basics for people to eat provides sustenance. But these tactics do not necessarily create a feeling of satisfaction—a necessary component of living a fulfilled life. Satisfaction is both a response and a reward for the labor, creativity, and care that goes into creating nourishment. At the seminar, an attendee asked what satisfaction looks like. I thought this was a great question, particularly because so much of living under capitalism means living in a constant state of dissatisfaction. We are constantly told we should want more, but when it comes to those who are struggling, they're told that their suffering is their fault, regardless of the many macro-level forces that rig the game in favor of those who already have more than enough. Capitalism, a double-headed beast, encourages overconsumption as a pathway to happiness but punishes poor and working-class people in particular for daring to even pursue happiness.

Understanding and cultivating true satisfaction is key to creating a world where we all have enough. Satisfaction is "the 'itis," a term used by Black folks to describe a feeling that is more than just being full of food. It's a post-meal feeling that makes you suck in a deep breath, rub your belly, and sink into the urge to close your eyes and slow down. It is the way a matriarch's lips curl into a smile when someone compliments her food. It is how reunion organizers survey the gathering and with a nod or a click of their teeth say, "This is good." Satisfaction, then, is a feeling of completeness, of knowing your gifts are appreciated, of knowing your hard work is not in vain. It doesn't mean everything is perfect—something always goes wrong, and someone always complains. It means that even as structures continue to threaten Black life at every turn, at the moment, this is, I am, we are, good.

How can this feeling, and this safety, be extended throughout our food system? How can more people feel satisfaction like this? Satisfaction is a pathway toward the outcomes we want to see, not a deterrent. What reunions teach us is that perhaps we can and should learn from the afterglow of eating and what makes people feel truly nourished. Dara Cooper, cofounder of the NBFJA and longtime food justice activist, always says that we have to make our movements sexy and irresistible—and tasty! Settings that are welcoming and familiar, leadership and vision that come from within communities that are deeply impacted by food injustice, foods that are culturally significant—these are but a few ways that food justice movements could live up to the mandate Cooper gave us. In other words, our work should resemble a family reunion. By taking satisfaction seriously, we'll attract more curiosity from those we want to serve. Reunions teach us how to be together in joy. But what does togetherness look like when we're grieving or suffering?

CHAPTER 3

REPASTS

———

Somehow, my sister has become the bearer of bad news in our family, ever since she was the person who told me that our grandmother died while I was halfway around the world in South Africa. So, when she called out of the blue one summer day in 2021, I had a feeling that once again she was going to tell me something that would alter my world. She asked me if I had heard about LaToya. I grew up alongside my cousin LaToya, and she had been a steady presence in my life even when I was sometimes adrift. She had died, my sister said, as I had sensed she would.

I was crushed. It felt as though the world I knew—one that had not been kind to LaToya but had somehow always kept us connected—had come crashing down. Shrouded in grief and disbelief, I headed back to Texas for the mourning rituals that Black studies professor Christina Sharpe terms "ordinary notes of care"—the everyday ways we choose to lean into connection in precarious or difficult moments.

At the funeral service, I was numb. This was August 2021. We were all figuring out the post-vaccine Covid landscape. Masks were required, and we were still hesitant to hug. I watched with detached curiosity as an usher sprayed Lysol above people's heads while we settled into the pews. I busied myself with my phone, texting a friend to describe how disembodied I felt, while I rehearsed the remarks I was to give. No one asked me any questions. It felt like there was nothing to say. I—like them—was there to bear witness to a life lost too soon. I was simply one of many who was using the solemn music, hope-filled sermon, and humor-laced reflections on Toya's life as an excuse to go inward. I remember few details about the funeral itself. The choir sang a hymn, but I don't remember what it was. Two preachers read scriptures from the Old and New Testaments. The choir sang again, and someone read a list of resolutions—expressions of sympathy from churches, businesses, our graduating class, and others. There was another song, and then it was time for me to give my remarks.

Whenever I have to speak in public, my biggest fear is that I will trip and fall on the way to the podium. But that wasn't my fear that day. My fear was that, despite what I had written, I wouldn't have anything to say at all—that grief would strip the words from me. I stepped to the microphone, greeted everyone, and read the words I had written, which included:

> Octavia Butler's novel *Parable of the Sower* is one of my favorites. In it, Laura Olamina leads a group of people toward freedom. Her gift, which sometimes is also a burden, is her ability to feel things deeply. She can feel others' joy and pain as if they are her own. In her pursuit of freedom, she writes Earthseed, a collection of tenets and instructions for how to create and sustain new life in new worlds. One of those tenets reads: "All that you touch you Change. All that you Change Changes you. The only last-

ing truth is Change. God Is Change." I do not know if LaToya ever read *Parable of the Sower*, though I would not be surprised if she did. What I do know is that—like Laura Olamina—Toya's ability and willingness to shapeshift from intellectual, to protector, to visionary, to athlete, to fashionista, to hype woman was possible because she felt and connected deeply with others and understood that through those feelings and connections, she was changed. All that touched Toya changed her. All of us whom she touched are forever changed too.

I walked straight from the podium, out the back door of the sanctuary, and to the bathroom. Grief washed over me. But I still couldn't cry.

At the repast, everything was different. There was less internal processing, less overwhelming grief, and more invitations—perhaps insistence—to be present with others. There, the focus was less about mourning Toya's death and more about nourishing the living with laughter, fond memories, and food.

There were actually two repasts. The one at the church immediately after the service was open to everyone, and in true Black funeral tradition, this was where most food was instructed to be sent. I didn't stick around for that one, choosing instead to follow Toya to her final resting place, a cemetery just outside of town. While my father offered scripture and prayers at the gravesite, volunteers in the church's reception hall organized food that people would carry away on Styrofoam plates. While my father recited, "We therefore commit this body to the ground, earth to earth, ashes to ashes, dust to dust; in sure and certain hope of the Resurrection to eternal life," someone back at the church shouted directions for what to serve, when, and to whom. While my father and all those gathered kept watch over the dead as her physical body journeyed six feet under, volunteers at the church kept watch over the living, making sure that all who wanted to be nourished would be.

The second repast was at my aunt's house, the backdrop for so many of my memories with Toya. In middle school, stretched diagonally across the bed in her room at the back of the house, we sketched out plans for our futures. A skilled basketball player, she wanted to have a career in the newly formed WNBA. Sometimes we dreamed of doing that together, though I was neither as skilled nor as interested in that path as she was. In high school, we schemed our way into rides to Stephen F. Austin State University, an hour away, to watch their women's basketball team. Photos in my high school photobook show us posing with players in their locker room. Our senior year, we both chose to go to prom alone. Before the dance, we posed in my aunt's front room—me wearing a shimmery ombré of blues and she a black dress that sparkled when she turned. Out front, the small but manicured yard was where we took our last selfie together three months prior to her death—a quick snap before I headed back to Austin and she headed to the local lake to hang out with family.

As I sat in the front room, the other mourners asked about my life—Where do you live now? Do you like it there? *DOCTOR* Reese! We're so proud of you!—the kind of comments that make me shy and uncomfortable. Being home meant reckoning with how little time I spent there. People didn't know me anymore, and I didn't know them, at least not like I used to.

Funerals, or homegoing celebrations, beckon people to return. These gatherings compel people back to the places that shaped them and, often, to scenes of discord to rebuild fractured relationships. In contexts like these, people who have not spoken in years find themselves sharing space, bridging gaps between "I remember when" and the present. The two most significant deaths I have experienced—that of my sister-cousin and that of my mother's mother—were both invitations to return and engage with home differently. I had moved several times and remained only superficially tethered to the place that raised me. I'd spent my twenties and most of my thirties hopscotching across class lines and figuring out a new sense of self in response to my dislocation. At these repasts, people welcomed me back into the fold, reminding me that if there was ever any doubt, home is always a place that can hold me and the contradictions I so desperately wanted to work through. Perhaps that is one of the central offerings of repasts.

Outside, some of the men set up folding tables, one of which would eventually host a game of dominoes. They pulled out coolers with drinks that wouldn't have been appropriate for the church repast, and some wore white "RIP" T-shirts with a portrait of Toya on the front. More than an acknowledgment of one's life, RIP T-shirts are a memorial in themselves, a ritual no less significant than the funeral. According to cultural and literary analyst Robin Brooks, they're another tether between the living and the dead, a coping mechanism for processing and living through grief in sartorial form.

At Toya's repast, I did what I always do when I can do nothing else: I served. I unwrapped platters of food, heated beans on the stove, and searched for serving utensils. Here we were, family serving family. One by one, we carried dish after dish outside until there was no space. The tables held so much food: baked and fried chicken, beans, greens, and more. One table was covered with nothing but desserts. It seemed like everyone in attendance wanted to drop off a little something.

While I was serving, a woman in line who was both surprising and familiar said, "You probably don't remember me." There was no way that I could forget her: Tasha. "I do," I replied. "You were one of her best friends." My cousin spent a brief time living in Dallas when we were teenagers. She met a fellow hooper, and I'd worried that Tasha would replace me. Now, we smiled and exchanged some quick words about how we were doing before she found a place to sit. Moments like that—when you encounter someone you haven't seen in nearly two decades—remind you that even tenuous connections are still that: connections.

I watched Toya's mom move around, greeting everyone. At the funeral, she was bereft and could hardly speak when offering her gratitude to attendees. At the repast, she had a different temperament. Grief wasn't the only emotion in the space. She laughed and hugged people who came to see about her. She exuded pride when she introduced her friends and colleagues who had traveled from Dallas to be with her. When I finished serving, she wanted me to meet all of them. She apologized for not addressing me by my formal title in the funeral program. "I'm not Dr. Reese here," I insisted. "I'm just Shanté." Then she introduced me to each person and shared stories about how inseparable Toya and I used to be. She told me how proud of me she was. The repast breathed life back into her. Being in that space—a cacophony of familiar sounds, no shortage of food, and unlimited care—gave her permission to smile and hope, if only for that moment. Even more than that, the loss itself, perhaps one of the most profound of her life, was, as Black feminist theorist Jennifer Nash wrote, "a precondition of being together," providing each of us an opportunity to relate to life, death, and one another differently.

Offering food to bereaved families is a longstanding tradition across regions and cultures, perhaps because when all else fails, food communicates things that are otherwise inexpressible. In *Consuming Passions: A Food-Obsessed Life*, memoirist Michael Lee West wrote, "Food knows all languages. It says, I know you are inconsolable. I know you are fragile right now. And I am so sorry for your loss. I am here if you need me . . . It is concern and sympathy in a Pyrex bowl. In the kindest sort of way it reminds us that life continues, that we must sustain and nourish it. Funeral cuisine may be an old custom, but it is the ultimate joining of community and food—it is humanity at its finest."

The word *repast* literally means "meal," but before I became a food studies scholar, the only way that I had ever seen the word used was by Black folks referring to a post-funeral meal. The repast, or "repass," is as much a part of a funeral ritual as the service itself. Church fellowship halls, community centers, backyards, and porches are transformed into spaces of care in which friends, community members, and distant relatives organize to ensure that the bereaved family is well fed, attended to, and surrounded by love.

Some writers and scholars write about "funeral food" as a Southern tradition. West has gone so far as to call it a Southern small-town tradition that is intimately tied to the church. She wrote that in church lingo it is "food for the bereaved," and thus, "when it comes to good funeral food, it all depends on how many good cooks are in the congregation." Social scientist Joshua Graham made a similar claim about funeral food being a Southern tradition, emphasizing that many of the mostly women who organize and provide food at church-based meals after a funeral do it because "it is just the Christian thing to do."

However, offering food in the context of bereavement is a nearly universal experience. From the United Kingdom to Greece, funeral foods are deeply significant to Christian concepts of mortality, memory, and the afterlife. In Kandiga, a community in northeast Ghana, funeral rites that include animal slaughter are so important that they persist despite concerns for how the practice increases food insecurity because families stretch themselves thin to purchase the foods required for the ritual. In Sri Lanka, Mala Batha is a meal served to families and all who come to pay their respects to the dead. As soon as someone dies, community members collect money and food items to contribute to the meal, which is cooked in the family's home whenever possible. It seems that no matter where you go in the world, food and death have an intimate relationship. In Black traditions, a repast becomes a stand-in for an entire experience beyond feeding the physical (living) body. To understand the significance, it is essential to place repasts within the context of Black funeral traditions more broadly. Commonly referred to as homegoings or celebrations of life, Black funerals are about both mourning and celebration. The name "homegoing" gestures toward an afterlife, a "something more" to come for the deceased.

For many Black communities, the food offered after a funeral or during the bereavement process is one way to understand communal care, Black sacred spaces, and lessons for those of us who continue to live in this world. The food is as important as the stories people tell about those who have passed on or the conversations that take place during the repast. The quality and quantity of food is an expression of respect for the bereaved family. It's also a commentary on the people bringing it. A repast is an opportunity for people to offer their best. It isn't the time to try a new dish. "Who fried the chicken?" and "Who made the potato salad?" are important questions as those in charge decide which food items are served at the public repast and which items are good enough to go home to the family. In a tongue-in-cheek way, literary scholar Karla FC Holloway proclaimed, "Bringing store-bought food to the house was once sure to invite a cynical aside and a 'tsk! tsking!' from those who knew better and expected that you should as well." Showing up empty-handed is a cardinal sin.

If the funeral service is primarily a space for mourning, then the repast might be characterized as a space for celebration, play, and laughter. In an essay in which she referenced her cousin's funeral, anthropologist Haile Eshe Cole wrote about the repast as a total transformation of space and energy: "Against the back wall was a line of long rectangular white tables connected end-to-end and covered with a variety of delicious foods: chicken wings, casseroles, green beans, potato salad, macaroni and cheese, cookies, pound cake, pies. Behind the table, five or so women in aprons prepared plates and served food to the growing line of people waiting to eat. I could see smiles. I could even hear laughter. Glancing around, one might never guess the proceeding and mournful string of events that reunited everyone that day." In Cole's experience, the food, women's labor, smiles, and laughter coalesced to usher mourners into the next phase of honoring their loved one. In my experience, the repast gives us permission to expand our sense of what mourning means; to allow grief to make room for other feelings. The repast offers an opportunity to lean into the fullness of complex emotions, even if they feel contradictory. A primary space for storytelling, we might imagine the repast as a space that expands with every memory shared, every joke told, every hug exchanged, and every promise to continue to look out for one another. Grief gives way to her oft-present traveling companion: joy. Perhaps the repast echoes a well-worn scripture that I've heard offered as a point of solace time and time again at funerals: "Weeping may endure for a night, but joy comes in the morning."

In a metaphorical sense, "the morning" is a meal, particularly the care and community that goes into making it. The joy is the stories and memories, which are often the highlight of the gathering itself. At Toya's repast, there was little talk about the circumstances of her death, how young she was, or how much we'd miss her—all things that lingered in the backs of our minds, or at least mine. The meal and the people right in front of us forced us to be present. We couldn't dwell on questions we couldn't answer, and there was no time to speculate about the future. Instead, we reveled in stories about her style, her basketball skills, and the many silly things we did together as teenagers. Hearing others talk about how funny she was or how smart she was or how she'd helped them through a difficult time filled me with pride. One by one, each story made her presence palpable—a person, a being more than the words we'd written in an obituary or said at her funeral service; a person, a being that transcended death itself. People, mostly men, drank from red solo cups over cards and dominoes, talking about how this is exactly the kind of party she'd want. Laughter filled the carport well into the evening. If nothing else, the repast kept us tethered to the moment and one another. Grief was near, but was only one guest among many that evening.

In a world that's increasingly isolated, traditions like repasts offer us glimpses into what care and connection look like when we gather around those who are suffering. Grief is an inescapable part of the human experience. But understandably, we take every opportunity to ignore and distance ourselves from pain. Corporations try to sell us ways to reduce suffering for ourselves and others. Unlike gadgets, self-help books, or diets that may encourage us to bypass suffering by focusing on quick-fix pathways to happiness, rituals like repasts require us to gather right in the middle of it. These rituals give us a chance to practice being with death, something that is deeply uncomfortable for many, especially in the US. To be with another's suffering and to be intentional with trying to alleviate it emphasizes shared humanity that isn't based on everything going well or everyone being happy. Instead, the repast unites us around a universal fact: every person dies, and when she does, someone will be left with an unimaginable loss that they can't bear alone. A repast says: you don't have to. In this context, it doesn't matter how much or how little someone eats. What matters most is that someone cares that they do. It matters that someone is paying attention to the needs of those who are hurting.

REPASTS ARE OFTEN THOUGHT of as offerings to people we know or are somehow connected to. They are a way to provide some respite for grieving families. But what happens when a whole city is mourning? Can the repast be imagined as a broader practice of community care? These aren't questions I'd considered until I met Chef Tam Patterson, the owner of Underground Café in Memphis, who organized a dozen businesses to provide a repast after the killing of Tyre Nichols.

On January 7, 2023, twenty-nine-year-old Tyre Nichols was pulled over, dragged from his car, and severely beaten by five police officers in Memphis. Three days later, he died. The official cause of death was listed as blunt force trauma to the head. At the time of Nichols's assault, only a week had passed since Keith Murriel, a forty-one-year-old Black man, died in police custody in Jackson, Mississippi, after being tased several times in the back of a police car. A mere ten days after Nichols's death, Darryl Williams, a thirty-two-year-old Black man in Raleigh, North Carolina, died in police custody after being tased three times, despite disclosing to officers that he had a heart condition. Nichols's death was part of the unrelenting refrain of Black death at the hands of the state that sometimes feels both expected and unending.

Nichols's death hit me particularly hard. In addition to my ongoing weariness at the assaults on Black life, Memphis was close to my heart. My first full-time academic job, in 2014, was at Rhodes College, a small, overwhelmingly white, private liberal arts school in the middle of the overwhelmingly Black city. Moving back and forth between white Rhodes and Black Memphis was difficult. I had lived in places where contradictions and racism thrived, but Memphis was different for me, as both a community member and a scholar of food studies.

In 2010, the Food Research and Action Center (FRAC) released a report that identified Memphis as "the hunger capital of the US" with a food insecurity rate of 26 percent. Memphis, like Baltimore, has a Black population that exceeds 60 percent. Like Baltimore, many of those residents are poor or working-class, and 22.5 percent of Memphians live below the poverty line—a figure that is double the national average. When people think of food insecurity, they may imagine emaciated, undernourished bodies. However, research has consistently shown that food insecurity and obesity are closely linked, especially for women in the US. Though researchers are still trying to understand the underlying mechanisms that fuel this conundrum, many suggest that poverty and lack of access to fresh, healthy, and affordable food is a contributing factor. Given this, it should be no surprise that Memphis experienced high rates of both. Memphis, like many cities in the US, is a place where there is no debating the presence and impact of anti-Blackness. Unarmed Nichols, treated as a threat though he posed no obvious one, became another example of how deadly that reality is. After his murder, I was mourning and so were others who were much closer to him. As in the aftermath of Freddie Gray's murder, people were also demanding justice.

During a press conference before bodycam footage documenting the assault on Nichols was released, the Memphis police chief called his death "a failing of basic humanity" and urged the public to temper their responses and to not resort to violence. A request for peaceful protest also came from Nichols's family. Many people—Memphians, political pundits, and those watching from around the country—expected violent protests reminiscent of what had happened in Baltimore after Freddie Gray's murder in 2015. Much of the city was on edge.

On January 27, the Memphis Police Department released over thirty minutes of camera footage that confirmed that Nichols was unarmed and that the officers took turns dealing blows that would ultimately lead to his death. Even more harrowing to me, as I watched only three minutes of the video, was that this didn't happen in an empty parking lot or on an abandoned street. Nichols was assaulted in a residential neighborhood, reportedly two minutes from his home. I wondered if the residents at the corner of Castlegate Lane and Bear Creek, beckoned by the lights from the police cars at the scene, watched in horror or curiosity.

A wave of activism in and beyond Memphis ensued. *NBC News* reported that at least seventeen protests erupted within hours of the release of the bodycam footage. Protesters shut down Interstate 55. Others gathered for a candlelight vigil at Tobey Skate Park, where Nichols used to skate. Across the US, people connected their local struggles against police violence to Nichols's murder and a broader call for police defunding and abolition.

While many protested, Tamra "Chef Tam" Patterson, a Memphis-based chef and the owner of Chef Tam's Underground Café, channeled her sadness, rage, and exasperation into a community-wide repast. Chef Tam had met Nichols's mother, RowVaughn Wells, soon after his death. She offered her hand for a handshake, but Wells refused it, choosing to pull her in for a hug instead. "I hugged her like, I mean, it was one of the tightest hugs you could imagine," Chef Tam remembered. It was a moment between two mothers of Black sons—one who was experiencing the worst and one who carried the fear that she could be in the same position one day. Chef Tam wanted to honor all that by creating a healing space for a family and a city that badly needed it.

Nichols's murder drew national and international attention, and the family anticipated his homegoing would be attended by hundreds of people—not only family and friends but also people from out of town. Chef Tam's restaurant was one of the largest in the city, so it would be perfect. This repast would have to be big enough to host a large crowd but intimate enough to not feel like a spectacle. Amid the ongoing unrest, other restaurant owners were afraid of what could happen to their businesses. They lamented how much money they'd lose if the city erupted into protests. Chef Tam countered with the grim reality that while these restaurant owners worried about their businesses, she worried about what could happen to her son in a country plagued by racist policing. "I have a teenage son," she told them. "I've got to tell my son how to act and present himself in public yet again so he's not killed by the police." Her vulnerability with her peers turned out to be an invitation. Many of those restaurant owners started asking a different question: What can we do to support?

Thirteen restaurants donated food for the repast. Chef Tam's restaurant provided Black American staples: roasted chicken, catfish, macaroni and cheese, sweet potato casserole, and collard greens. Chef Kelly English of The Second Line and Restaurant Iris donated red beans and rice. The Beauty Shop restaurant made turkey and gravy with cranberry chutney. Felicia Suzanne's sent deviled eggs, while Tsunami offered chicken satay with Thai peanut sauce. McEwen's provided cheese grits—a Southern delicacy. Rendezvous laid out sausage and cheese platters. Cocozza offered lasagna. Acre Restaurant donated sweet potato and sausage hash. Muddy's Bake Shop, Ecco, and Sunrise rounded out the offerings with pastries and other desserts. The restaurants—some Black-owned, others not—participated in the long-held tradition of feeding bereaved families after a funeral. No one was under the illusion that food could replace this son of Memphis. But by operating within this sacred tradition, Chef Tam recognized something else: that by extending an invitation to others, they could perform the sacred acts of witnessing, serving, and nourishing.

The citywide support from other restaurateurs freed Chef Tam to focus on how she wanted the repast to feel. According to those who knew and loved Nichols, photography was his happy place. So Chef Tam downloaded several of his photos and had them printed on canvases. Her husband drove through ice and snow to the only open Walgreens to pick them up. In a private room reserved for the immediate family, she set up those photos so that they could be surrounded by their loved one's life and not only his death. One photo captured the Hernando deSoto Bridge straddling the Mississippi River set against a darkening red and orange sky. Another showcased a close-up of train tracks at the place where rails met gravel. As a mother, as a person who had lost people in her own family, Chef Tam wanted to create an atmosphere that emphasized that Nichols's life mattered.

Chef Tam and her colleagues took a well-known, beloved tradition of supporting bereaved families and transformed it into a practice of community care at a larger scale. Memphis was in a state of collective grief. Nichols's murder was yet another moment in which people in Memphis and beyond recognized that the failures to protect Black life are built into the systems that we're taught are supposed to keep us safe and nourished. In these moments, we see clearly that we cannot cede the soul and community-saving work of nourishment to the state or capitalist institutions. We must imagine otherwise.

I grew up among Black people who understood that their time of need would come. They embodied a scripture I heard countless times during the offering at church: "Give, and it will be given to you. A good measure, pressed down, shaken together and running over, will be poured into your lap. For with the measure you use, it will be measured to you." What Chef Tam pulled together is an excellent case study of how to extend the "we" outward, to widen our embrace to include people who are not "ours"—as in, our family, our friends, our immediate community. Chef Tam looked at Tyre Nichols's mother and saw herself. She didn't know her personally, but she knew what it was like to be a mother of a Black son she couldn't fully protect. She had an intimate relationship with her own fear about her newly licensed teenage son driving alone—the restlessness, the angst. She empathized. Her empathy moved her to action, to be of service. Perhaps more than any other type of gathering, repasts invite us to not just sympathize but empathize with others.

Those lessons of empathy, widening our circle, drawing on tradition, and gathering despite difficult emotion are necessary tactics to further food justice. Any pursuit of justice must have space to hold both grief and joy: grief for the many losses that accumulate every second that injustice goes unfettered, and a deeply embodied joy that comes from knowing that each being has a shot at living a nourished life.

FOUR MONTHS AFTER I attended their family reunion in Washington, D.C., in 2023, Sharon and Toni, sisters who lovingly nicknamed me "the people's anthropologist," called me. They informed me that their mother had passed away and that other deaths in the family had followed. From gathering with their family for celebratory reunions in Maryland and D.C. to gathering for burials, life had made a complete circle. Sharon said, "Thank you for thinking of us in our time of sorrow. Your current research is so important to our culture. We have been to numerous funerals and homegoing celebrations in the last few months. Each holding our family rituals in their own way." I felt the ache of knowing that, in a seemingly random act of fate, I was now a steward of some of this family's stories. It was, and is, a sacred responsibility.

Sharon's message reiterates the significance of repasts and post-funeral gatherings in the simplest way: rituals are important to cultures and families, and that significance extends beyond the food itself. Though there were tons of food at Toya's repast, I don't remember eating any of it. I spent most of my time serving, talking, and remembering—forms of nourishment that accompanied the food. This kind of labor—the work to make sure everyone feels cared for and supported—undergirds many types of gatherings. It is uncompensated, often gendered, and understood to be part of what it means to be in community with others.

Repasts, like family reunions, make space for us to remember and to be together. But I cannot emphasize enough how important it is to have these gatherings as a place to be with our own and others' suffering. In Western societies in particular, we struggle with the reality of death. Repasts are one of the few rituals we have to practice sitting with loss. Perhaps even more than a funeral itself, repasts insist that we *live* with loss even if we succumb to the weight of it temporarily. When we gather for repasts, we wrap our arms around one another in an attempt to share some of that weight. Part of food justice is sharing in the risks and benefits of the food system, as I talked about in the introduction. To do that, we need a lot of practice with willingly sharing burdens that aren't "ours" but will make life easier for someone else. We cannot live into the fullness of a "we" or community without it.

I have been on both sides of repasts. I've served grieving families, and I've received the care of being served. What I know from both experiences is that, at its core, a repast is a practice of reciprocity that requires an openness to give and receive. To receive care from others in a time of sorrow is vulnerable. Your grief is laid bare. The reality that you do not fully control life's outcomes or timing makes itself known in tears, wails, and hugs. Your efforts to keep on living, to keep your loved one's name and legacy alive, are tenacious. It is one thing to be seen by others. It is an entirely different thing to be witnessed, to allow others to join the process of piecing together life after death simply by being there. To give care is a sacred responsibility and honor. As one who bears witness to others' pain and joy, you reflect to the bereaved that there is space for them; that they are worthy of being cared for; that the world will slow down and honor their loved one, if only for a moment. To bear witness in this way is to also affirm your own humanity, to surrender to the reality that today it is someone else; tomorrow it may be you. Repasts remind us that we take care of one another. We got us.

CHAPTER 4

MUTUAL AID

———

Two events set the tone for my new life in Austin and how I've come to understand and practice care: the Covid-19 pandemic when I moved there in 2020 and Winter Storm Uri in mid-February 2021. There had been reports that a winter storm was heading toward us. We were encouraged to stock up on essentials and hunker down. We were expecting extremely cold temperatures, plus maybe a little ice and snow were expected. Most people were preparing to stay inside, but few were worried. Local schools and universities took precautions, canceling classes and limiting the number of staff who needed to work on site. As someone new to the university trying to catch her breath, the canceled classes were music to my ears.

Around 1:30 a.m. on February 15, I woke up to a power outage. I wasn't the only one. Local power companies had started rolling blackouts the night before, beginning with the eastern part of the city where I lived, in an attempt to preserve energy and "save the grid." However, the blackouts didn't roll. While neighborhoods like mine on the east side of Austin experienced power outages, others never lost power at all. In the early hours of Monday morning, maps showing which neighborhoods had power and which ones did not emerged on social media, along with critical analysis revealing that most neighborhoods without power were heavily populated by Black and Brown residents.

Though local energy companies had expected the storm, little proactive work had been done to fortify Texas's electric grid. In a recording, the owner of a Texas-based natural gas company boasted about the revenue that would result from the unprecedented use of energy by households to stay warm. City officials and others quickly explained that it was not racism that dictated who had power and who did not; it was the fact that power to critical resources like hospitals was not cut, and homes and businesses that shared those grids were the lucky ones. The irony is, of course, that the built environment and access to critical resources like hospitals are already racialized. The power outages, subsequent water and food shortages, and millions of dollars in damage across the city and state were the result of ongoing neglect that disproportionately impacted Black and Brown neighborhoods. As many scholars and activists have pointed out, the language of "natural" disaster only serves to mask the systematic ways that colonialism, anti-Blackness, and public policy create conditions of vulnerability.

I started to worry as I felt the temperature in my apartment drop into the sixties. Not knowing how long the blackouts would last, I searched for hotels with availability. Hotels that were normally $100–200 a night were triple and quadruple that price. Online booking was disabled for many hotels. Others were not answering their phones or had long wait times. After over an hour and with the help of two friends—one searching and making calls from

Honduras—I secured hotel rooms for myself and my Covid podmate, Bedour.

The next challenge would be getting there. The streets around my building were sheer ice. There were so few winter service vehicles to move ice and snow that only the major thoroughfares were cleared. The cars that were on the road tried to follow the tracks of previous cars, hoping that the grooves might give them more traction. I carefully followed suit. What would have normally been a two-minute drive to Bedour's apartment took almost twenty minutes—not the least of which was me alternating between holding my breath and praying that drivers wouldn't spin out when we made turns on the streets-turned-ice rinks. After living in Washington, D.C., for five years, I trusted my own ability to drive in snow and ice. What I didn't trust was the poor infrastructure and the resolve of other panicked drivers.

After I picked up Bedour, we continued our trek. At the hotel, it took thirty minutes to find a parking spot and then another hour of standing in line to check in. The hotel restaurant was shut down, so the only food we had were the snacks I'd hurriedly packed in a bag before leaving my house. But I didn't care about any of that. We were warm and safe. We were among the lucky ones, an uncomfortable reality that I had a difficult time sitting with.

Hungry and anxious from the multiple hours it had taken to complete an ordinarily ten-minute drive, I laid across the bed, unsettled by the whole ordeal: the lack of infrastructure, the dangerous streets, the fact that the thing that separated me from others who didn't have heat or power was economic privilege, flexibility with my time, and a community of friends who had the same. I was grateful for warmth and safety, but I wasn't content. After tweeting a few criticisms of the city and state's lack of preparedness, I decided that I would do what my friends had done for me. Using social media, I put out a call: Who needs help? Who's willing to share resources and/or warm space with others? Tweets and Facebook messages started to trickle in. As soon as I'd get one, I'd retweet it, asking who could meet the need. Soon, a few dozen messages swelled to hundreds with requests from all over the state. Others jumped in. Bedour began tweeting, and so did our colleague Ashley, a person who would ultimately become one of my closest friends because of this experience. Aaron, a fellow anthropologist and colleague, messaged me on Twitter to ask if we needed help, and I said yes. We didn't have a system for tracking requests, so he created a spreadsheet. Soon, my inbox was filled with others who wanted to help.

Using WhatsApp, we coordinated self-care check-ins, grocery store runs, and cooking hot meals in the kitchens of those who still had power or gas. For the next five days, about three dozen of us—most of whom had never met—collected money, groceries, and food to redistribute to people who were facing all kinds of emergencies. There were requests for rides to pharmacies to pick up life-saving medications. When my own power returned after two days, I prepared huge pots of beans and soup and offered my couch to others who needed somewhere to stay. There were requests for warm places for elders, milk and baby formula, water, and money to replace items lost due to burst pipes. As each request came in, someone would serve as a contact person, making sure that whoever was in need was met with a friendly, patient voice on the other end of the phone call or text. We tracked what time a request came in, who was assigned to meet it, and when it was complete.

Mutual aid—a model for meeting people's needs in ways that emphasize mutuality over charity—was a saving grace in Austin and beyond. Established organizations like the Austin Justice Coalition (AJC), Communities of Color United (CCU), and Black Mamas ATX were also on the ground, meeting as many needs as possible. As we got requests from outside Austin, we forwarded them to organizers we'd met online due to the crisis. Hundreds of requests came from people in Houston, so Aaron created a spreadsheet for organizers there. Together, our ragtag crew and these groups demonstrated something we all desperately needed to see and experience together: that ultimately, our collective efforts could make a world of difference, especially during an unprecedented disaster.

Organizing mutual aid in a city I'd only lived in for about seven months was not exactly on my bingo card when I started at UT-Austin. Because of the pandemic and teaching online, I'd met few of my colleagues and even fewer people outside the university. Though the circumstances were not ideal, stepping up in that moment gave me an opportunity not only to do good in the city I'd come to call home but also to work alongside colleagues and strangers. Mutual aid did this for me, for us; it was my introduction to Austin. I learned more about the city's bureaucracy, layout, and the state of community-led safety needs in those five days than I had or have at any other point. It provided an opportunity to practice meeting people's needs in real time, an opportunity to practice communalism and trust with fewer barriers to connections. Yes, there were obstacles: snow, ice, no electricity, unstocked shelves. But operating as an impromptu mutual aid collective—not a government agency, not a nonprofit—meant that bureaucracy was not one of them. During large-scale disruption, we practiced freedom through giving largely outside of capitalistic exchange, a value that I'd like to see grow. There are many ways to respond to disaster—greed and self-preservation among them. But there is also collective care. There's creativity, and there's leveraging good fortune and privilege to make someone else's life more bearable. What does it mean that, during Winter Storm Uri, we chose to come together?

Sometimes, mutual aid is misunderstood as simply a response to emergency, but it is much more than crisis management. Anarchist philosopher Peter Kropotkin reasoned that mutual aid is part of our evolutionary impulse because we are drawn toward connection and care for one another. But with the emergence of the modern state, many people have embraced individualism over communalism. In our food system, individualism looks like self-checkout lanes that allow you to bypass engaging with cashiers—a potentially significant moment of exchange with someone outside your primary social circles. An individualistic mindset also fosters the expectation that whatever produce you desire is well stocked in the supermarket, with very little curiosity about the workers who make it possible for you to have it. Our individualism and alienation from the production of our food is a relatively recent development. However, our inherent desire to meet one another's needs has not been completely eradicated. As much as individualism is deeply engrained in Western societies, these values don't completely supplant our desire to help or build mutually beneficial systems. If they did, Kropotkin argued, human society would fail. We need only to follow the impulse to gather and put it into practice.

Kropotkin's theory of mutual aid was introduced over a century ago. Contemporary activists, organizers, and writers have taken it up as a framework for envisioning how to radically reorient our society, including our food systems. Mutual aid is a powerful way to self-organize—especially in times of ecological disaster or crisis that expose the state's inability (or unwillingness) to meet the needs of all people. Law professor and longtime community organizer Dean Spade has articulated three key elements of mutual aid projects: (1) meet people's basic survival needs while also building a clear, shared understanding of the conditions that create those needs; (2) mobilize people and expand solidarity; and (3) eschew the need for a savior by solving problems through collective action. When we were organizing during Winter Storm Uri, we didn't have these criteria at the top of mind, but they were present. Getting people food, water, medication, and cash was our top priority. While we did that, we fired off criticisms of the state on social media and afterward discussed the conditions that had led to the crisis. Each of us had a skillset that contributed to what we were able to accomplish. None of us were saviors. We were in it together.

Mutual aid as a political orientation informs how we care for one another, acknowledging that on some level there is always a crisis or emergency. As Kropotkin theorized, modern society shaped by capitalism chips away at our ability and willingness to work collectively to shape the conditions of our lives. In other words, the more we buy into competition, meritocracy, and the belief that we are not responsible for one another, the less likely we are to see helping our neighbors as connected to helping ourselves. While profitability was a primary concern for energy companies during Winter Storm Uri, for example, everyday people faced a real question of how (or if) they'd show up for their next-door neighbors or complete strangers who were struggling. Many, like the ones who were part of our collective, accepted the challenge to share their resources and reduce as much suffering as possible by not letting people face a crisis alone. Mutual aid gives us an orientation toward being *with* people and not just doing things *for* people—a fundamental difference between mutual aid and charity. The "being with" takes many forms.

Like Heber Brown's approach to gardening in Baltimore, which offered an alternative to charity, mutual aid offers us a way to practice relationship-making and capacity-building that aren't rooted in creating and maintaining hierarchies. A mutual aid philosophy minimizes surveillance and the policing of people's needs by simply believing them when they ask for something. When people requested cash from our collective, we didn't ask a lot of questions to verify their need, though we did keep track of who asked for what so that we could keep up with who'd already been served. Mutual aid also involves simply listening, rather than assuming what people need. I can't even recall how many times members of our collective sat on the phone with people as they cried, recounted their losses, or just reflected gratitude. Here, I call that listening. But anthropologist Deborah Thomas might call it "witnessing 2.0," an embodied practice that can lead to shifts in consciousness because of the intimacy and sense of responsibility that are built between the sharer and the listener.

At its core, mutual aid is based on the truth that because we are living under the precariousness of capitalism and in a society built through colonialism and violence, any one of us could be the person who is in need at any moment. If we take this understanding of mutual aid as a valuable way to orient ourselves toward meeting our own and others' needs, what does that mean for how we understand care, interdependence, and, dare I say, love?

Mutual aid collectives like the one I was part of during Winter Storm Uri come together in response to inequities in material conditions. In meeting people's needs, they're also shaping what we want the future to look like; they offer alternative ways to think about what it means to be in community, especially with people you don't know personally. Spade offered some useful, urgent questions for reorienting us toward collectivism: "How can we build the networks and methods and practices to provide the basic necessities for each other's survival as the disasters unfold and as much of the infrastructure crumbles or fails? And how can we dismantle the infrastructure designed to extract from and subdue us?" These are questions that should guide us in any pursuit of justice, including food justice.

Realistically, these questions aren't necessarily answered in moments of acute crises. When someone's calling because they need food or because their car is stuck in a ditch or their baby needs formula, that isn't the time to ponder how to build long-term infrastructure and practices. In the moment, we are just doing what we can to reduce suffering. It isn't perfect, and it isn't pretty. But it is necessary. After the acute crises of the winter storm were over—when the sun melted the ice and we were less sleep-deprived—we gathered to debrief. What lessons did we learn? What did we wish we'd done better? What did we learn about ourselves? On a video call, as some of us saw each other's faces for the first time, we reflected on what we'd experienced. We celebrated the over $50,000 we had raised and the hundreds of people we had supported. We lamented our limitations and cursed the city's failures. But mostly we gave thanks for one another and expressed how cool it was for a group of strangers to come together so quickly and relatively efficiently. We didn't know it when we started, but we became one of our own models for creating nourishment.

Mutual aid is a political strategy for building collective consciousness and community, but it isn't always viewed as political. Sometimes, it isn't even called mutual aid. While our efforts during Winter Storm Uri were political and in part driven by criticisms of the state, providing food, water, and funds to people impacted by a weather-related event wasn't seen as controversial. But other forms of mutual aid are controversial, particularly those that appear to directly challenge the state. Both are spurred by moral conviction, but when authority is directly challenged, debates about efficacy and the ethics of some efforts enter the conversation. Perhaps one of the more salient case studies is the growing movement for solidarity with Palestinians beginning in 2023, when war between Israel and Palestine commenced.

Spring 2024 was heartbreaking. On April 17, a few hours before the sun broke the horizon, students at Columbia University gathered tents, supplies, and allies on the university's South Lawn to set up what is considered the first student-led encampment in the US in response to genocide and escalating war in Palestine. Named the Liberated Zone, the encampment represented the students' commitment to forcing the university to divest from Israel. When the encampment entered its thirty-fourth hour, Columbia's then president, Minouche Shafik, authorized police to enter campus. Over one hundred students were arrested. Inspired and outraged by the police crackdown on Columbia's Liberated Zone, students across the country organized their own encampments and protests condemning genocide in Gaza. These universities were also the site of counterprotests from Zionist students and others, some of whom called the encampments and those who aligned with Palestinian liberation foolish, misinformed, or anti-Semitic. Over the coming days and weeks, people around the world watched as students at Columbia and other universities were assaulted, tased, tear-gassed, and arrested. As student-led encampments around the world became too many to count, university administrators scrambled to respond. Many times, the response was violent.

At UT–Austin, we watched in horror and anticipation. We knew that it was only a matter of time before the crisis was at our doorstep. Students at the university had been building consciousness and organizing in solidarity with Palestinians for a long time. Some faculty knew that should something pop off at UT, they'd need our support. Our group was made up of student organizers, a core group of faculty who had been organizing together for several years—some during Winter Storm Uri—and others who felt outraged by the violent responses occurring around the country. We all had different entry points into the fraught topic of the war in Gaza, but we were mostly united in the belief that we didn't want our campus to feel like a militarized war zone with students on one side and police on the other. We didn't know exactly what to do, but we knew we had to do *something*.

On the first day the police were called to disband students, I was on my way home from a spin class. I knew that there was a teach-in planned on the South Lawn. Students had organized a gathering that included food, music, poetry, and speakers to teach about Palestine and the political moment. That didn't seem to be something I needed to be present for. But before I could drop my keys on the counter, panicked texts and calls for faculty support came in a steady stream. There was an overwhelming police presence on campus, said colleagues, and it was growing. I quickly changed clothes, grabbed some cash, and left two phone numbers on the fridge for my partner—one for the Travis County jail and one for a colleague—before heading to campus.

The timing couldn't have been worse. Days before, UT–Austin's then president, Jay Hartzell, had announced that sixty people who were employed in DEI-related positions, the majority of whom were Black and Brown, were laid off. Hartzell had previously promised that no one would lose their job in response to the state-mandated ban on DEI offices and programming, but the ramifications of this ban were becoming clear. While some were protesting these firings, the police had been called to campus to quell a growing demonstration in support of Palestine.

I didn't know what to expect when I got to campus, but I am a student of history, so I know that overwhelming police presence rarely leads to anything good. On any other spring day, the South Lawn teems with students studying, chatting in small groups, tossing footballs, or napping. In the period between classes when students are hustling from one side of campus to the other, the expansive stretch of manicured grass is an informal meeting place. That day, the South Lawn looked nothing like I'd ever seen it. There were no erected tents, just a few blankets and personal belongings flung around. Many of the students looked bewildered, as if they'd been caught off guard, and it seemed they had. What was expected to be a teach-in had become a standoff with the police. Students huddled together, linked arms, and shouted at the dozen or so police officers in riot gear. They yelled as if they were fearless, but anyone near the frenzied energy could feel their fear.

On each side were counter-protesters—some students with Israeli flags joined by supporters who were not students, several of whom had brought their toddlers in strollers or on their hips. Behind them and scattered among them were reporters and camera crews, hungry to capture the next viral segment. Spectators were all around, close enough to see what was happening but far enough away to signal that they weren't part of the protest. Between the police, the media, and the bystanders, the students (who I am not sure had planned to be protesters) were surrounded. University leadership watched from the administration tower at the center of campus, surveying the landscape from their panopticon.

I was one of the first to arrive, along with Ashley, my colleague and friend who brought me food during Winter Storm Uri. Working through disaster bonded us. Since then, from shared late nights at the state capitol to backyard meetings with colleagues to imagine the future of universities, Ashley had become much more than a colleague. She was my family. If I had to face uncertainty with anyone, I'd choose her any day of the week.

In front of us we saw scared young people—some of whom were students in our classes. The only thing that made sense was to join them.

We entered the South Lawn and stood between the police and the students before linking arms with those on the front lines. I glanced to my left and my right, watching the students' resolve waver, unsure if they should hold their ground or retreat. I was unsure, too.

I faced the 300-pound Black police officer in front of me. We locked eyes, and I thought—despite my better judgment, despite all that I know about how "protect and serve" was being used to break dissenters, even though they were getting into formation—*surely this man is not going to run me over.*

Reader, I don't know if you've ever had another human armored in riot gear ram into you while you pray that you do not fall—the feeling of your muscles tightening to prepare for impact or the split second between the impact itself and your brain registering the blow. It was a first for me, and it was scary. The police regrouped, counted down from three to one, and pushed into us. I squeezed my eyes shut, held my breath, braced myself, and hoped to the universe that I didn't get trampled. They performed the same push several more times. Each time, I worried that my glasses would get knocked off. I clung tightly to Ashley. My five-foot-four frame makes me feel like a giant next to her five-foot-one. *I cannot let her fall*, I thought. I watched the police pluck people from the crowd at random, drag them out into the open, and zip-tie their hands behind their backs. *Oh my god, they're going to take us one by one.*

I released sighs of relief each time I didn't fall or get snatched. Rounds of deep breaths seemed to be the only thing standing between me and either jail or injury. As deep breaths gave way to shallower ones, I knew I was panicking: *I have to get out of this crowd.* I grabbed Ashley's arm, told her I felt like I was suffocating, and half-dragged her out of the center. But that wasn't before perhaps hundreds of photos had been taken. As I'd later learn, images of me and my friend were being posted online, and we would unintentionally become the faculty faces of UT–Austin's protests. When I arrived home that night, thankful that I had indeed made it home, I crawled into the corner of my couch and wept—for the students, for my colleagues, and for myself, knowing that the traumas I'd witnessed hadn't quite registered, and not knowing whether I'd be ready for them when they did.

Student- and faculty-led actions continued to unfold over the coming week. I, and others who were there on the first day of protests, continued to show up. University responses ranged from increasing police presence and more arrests to surveillance. During a second teach-in on the steps of the administration tower, institutional representatives watched while leaders shouted speeches in call-and-response form, a tradition where a speaker offers a statement or proclamation (the call) and the audience repeats it or another predetermined phrase (the response). Social justice movements have used this method at rallies as one way to keep people engaged and motivated. We were not allowed to have amplified sound during the teach-in; the call-and-response ritual ensured that new information was heard and understood by everyone participating. Through it all, mutual aid efforts kept us all going.

Groups mobilized quickly to fill specific needs as they arose. There was a team to aid in identifying who was arrested; a team to provide security at various events; a team to draft a statement to university leadership condemning the use of police force against students; a team to photograph and record violent interactions with the police; and a team to collect and pass out water and snacks at rallies and protests. Nearly anything you can think of as necessary to survive during uncertainty, we had it—everything except the guarantee that our jobs or bodies would be protected by the university or the state. In that vein, we had to operate under the mantra "We all we got."

Two efforts stand out to me as examples of the power of gatherings orchestrated around mutual aid: a cultivated care space and the jail support crew. As volunteers increased and as donations poured in, we created a central place for supplies and meeting. Along one wall of the room, we stacked case after case of water. Against another, two tables were set up to organize medical supplies. Another supported food—everything from fruit to granola to pans of salad, rice, and other food donated from other events or by organizations. At one point, a volunteer made a dash to the grocery store to make sure that we had some verified plant-based options for vegans. In the corner of the room, a colleague who could not be out in the protest crowds set up a quiet space with pillows, blankets, essential oils, and other comforts for anyone who was experiencing sensory overload. By turning a room in a building on the edge of campus into a distribution center, we created an extension of the liberated zones that were popping up around the country.

In the reporting that followed UT–Austin's protests, many questioned the commitment and knowledge of the students involved. In some cases, commentators went so far as to say that the students didn't know what they were doing; they were just following the crowd or joining the next Instagram-worthy moment. Perhaps there were some students who were looking to be the next TikTok sensation, but there were far more people with a lot to lose. Palestinian and Palestinian American students were continually harassed and surveilled even when the protests subsided. Other students of various racial and ethnic identities who were arrested later faced the possibility of expulsion from the university. Whether they knew the full extent of what they were stepping into, I can't say. But these students moved with a conviction that invited others to view life from the edge. Maybe we'd see that there's really no edge there; there are only the webs of connection that tether people, places, and our collective well-being. No matter how polarizing things get, no matter how far people are pushed from the center, there is no world where our actions don't impact one another.

Mutual aid is often—though not exclusively—imagined by people who are already on the margins of society. They occupy those margins for a host of reasons: racial or ethnic identity, sexuality, class, gender, and so on. Some might think this is because people on the margins have the most at stake, which compels them to engage in mutual aid to support themselves and others. I would like to think it is because those at the margins have more practice in activating the values that create the foundation for human and planetary survival: interdependence, collaborative decision-making, and resource- and wealth-sharing.

The student protests and mutual aid efforts that sprang up around the world in spring 2024 were examples of spontaneous mutual aid. These efforts were in response to immediate threats to an individual's or community's well-being. At UT–Austin, the bail funds, the volunteer medical support, and the makeshift kitchen and food distribution setups were coupled with political education. This model was aligned with a tradition that emphasizes that the difference between charity and mutual aid is the extent to which people are equipped with knowledge and skills to become self-determining. That tradition assumes that when their basic needs are met, people are better positioned to learn about and challenge oppressive structures that determine the haves and the have-nots.

In the case of student protests, mutual aid offers another important opportunity: for people to work out in real time what global solidarity and accountability means. It's a messy process. People fail. Political alliances across lines of difference can be fraught. People who enjoy privileges in this version of the world sometimes struggle with following the leadership of those who don't. On more than one occasion during my university's protests, I found myself on the giving *and* receiving ends of frustration. I became frustrated with the pace at which things moved, with criticisms from folks who had not been involved in the organizing, and with the well-intentioned suggestions that we might somehow reason with the university officials who were calling the cops on us. In those moments, frustration tested the belief that there's a place for everyone in movements.

The friction between frustration and belief challenged my commitment. But mutual aid is a meeting ground. It's the place where you're constantly reminded that your well-being is tethered to another's. This means that we really had to trust people's evaluation of their own capacities and contributions. It was just as important to honor and protect those in our crew who had sensitive immune systems or fraught visa statuses as it was to protect those embroiled in standoffs with the police. If we're not careful, we can assume that only those in the videos, images, and interviews are the heroes. But progress relies on many kinds of people. Mutual aid only works because of the sometimes-unseen labor of people who do grocery store runs, organize materials, manage donations, or otherwise keep group morale high. If freedom is not only an idea but a place that is created, then mutual aid is a practice of working out the conditions for all to inhabit it.

When we're all coming from different backgrounds and have different motivations, how do we make space for everyone—especially when tensions are high? When you're new to organizing, how do you find your space and the people whom you want to work alongside? These are two very big questions. Like the earlier one about building more care-filled infrastructures, these questions are hard to answer in frenzied moments. When you're facing imminent threats, most of the time, it's all hands on deck. But one lesson I took away from campus organizing was that no matter how fast things are moving, there must be space for stillness and quiet. If I'm honest, part of the reason why irritations ran high when we were strategizing or responding to the moment was because we were exhausted—physically and emotionally. We'd go from serving as faculty marshals protecting students to managing several threads of communications to dropping off food at the local jail to crowdsourcing bail support to . . . you get the picture. We were so connected, and things were moving so quickly, that at one point I suggested we pause all communication for a couple hours each day just so that we could let our nervous systems reset. Working at that pace for days on end is hard, and it isn't healthy—even when you're supporting a cause that you desperately believe in. It not only strains your body and your heart; it also strains your relationships. When I'd find myself being more impatient than normal, I knew that, at the very least, I needed a nap and a hug. As Tricia Hersey, founder of the anti-capitalist Nap Ministry, has proclaimed: "Rest is a form of resistance because it disrupts and pushes back against capitalism and white supremacy."

IMAGINE A WORLD WHERE—for the most part—everyone's needs are met. A world where people do not lock their doors because the community is such that everyone is protecting everyone's property as if it is their own. A world where people grow, harvest, cook, and share food in ways that are organic and do not require sign-up sheets or keeping tabs on who is doing what. A world where elders' and young people's ideas about interdependency are heralded as guiding lights in a dark world. In this version of a world, "ownership" translates to "stewardship," such that anything that belongs to me could very easily belong to you—not by force but by choice and consent. This might sound utopian. Perhaps it is in some ways. But it is also the world I grew up in—the world that informed my deep belief that mutual aid is a practice worth investing in.

When I was a child in Cooper Settlement, I did not understand that the cooperation that informed my daily life was a radical way of being in the world. In my mind, most of what living out in the country meant was inconvenience and slowness. The population of Crockett, the town we claim but weren't technically incorporated into, hovered around 7,400 during my formative years and has since declined to fewer than 7,000. For me, Cooper Settlement was where life waited to happen, where I waited for weekdays when I could go to school, where I waited out my high school years so I could scurry off to college. But, in reality, of course, it was where life happened. From neighbors sharing produce to a young person filling out bills for an elder who had Parkinson's and could not write, to the conversations about local politics and shared fates that I did not understand as a child—these daily acts of mutuality created a world within a world, a world in which, if the community could help it, no one would go without their needs being met.

Cooper Settlement is not like Austin. The life each affords me is quite different, though some of those early lessons back home inform how I choose to live in the city. They both illustrate the power of place-based, collective care that prioritizes the resources we do have over what we lack. Mutual aid is a spatial practice, meaning it takes place *somewhere*, and wherever it happens, it has the potential to transform those places. The *right* place is wherever your feet are planted. The *right* people are always among us. The *right* time is always now. A small, unincorporated community of Black folks whose ancestors were enslaved on the land where they continue to make homes: right place. A group of mostly strangers using the internet to organize resources for communities impacted by a winter storm: right people. A brave, if not also afraid, group of students, faculty, and staff holding their university accountable for its investments in violence months after the state abolished DEI programs in public institutions: right time. What I am trying to get you to understand, dear reader, is that the right anything is a home-grown experiment in world-building. If freedom is a place, as geographer and abolitionist Ruth Wilson Gilmore has repeatedly exclaimed, then mutual aid is one of the practices that creates it.

Mutual aid, alongside the other rituals and practices explored in this book, gives us a framework for closing the gap between "us" and "them." There's a reason why some forms of gathering—like protests—are discouraged and sometimes violently shut down. They're a threat to the status quo. Whenever we can see our struggles as shared, the closer we get to building (food) movements that honor one another's humanity as we pursue justice. Can you imagine the worlds we can build when we fully step into our collective power as a threat to an unjust food system?

CONCLUSION

GATHERING ON THE BRINK OF UNCERTAINTY

THE IDEA FOR this book was planted in November 2022 at a panel at the American Studies Association (ASA) annual conference in New Orleans, Louisiana. Our panel was called "Cook Out: Blackness with No Roof." I, along with my colleagues La Marr Jurelle Bruce, Jennifer DeClue, Hanna Garth, Bettina A. Judd, James P. Padilioni, J. T. Roane, and Savannah Shange, convened the panel to explore the cookout as a practice of Black community, Black conviviality, and Black creativity. My presentation was focused on communal eating as part of an infrastructure of care that includes feeding both the physical and social body while also (often) claiming a right to public space. To open my presentation, I did what any reasonable anthropologist who studies Black food culture would do: I played "Wobble," by V.I.C., asked the whole room to stand up, and danced on stage with my co-panelists. Spaces between chairs became our dance floor. For the next five minutes, we didn't care that we were in a session at an academic conference. We simply enjoyed a moment of being together—in all our similarities, differences, hopes, and grievances. It reflected the radical hospitality that is at the root of so many Black gatherings. We brought the cookout to academia. People came. No one was turned away.

Three months later, Caroline Adams, an editor at Norton, emailed me and asked if I'd be interested in writing a book about food and race. I said that if they wanted a book about anti-Black racism and food, I would need to recommend others. I had already done that—written mostly about what was wrong with the food system—and didn't have my sights on doing it again, at least not at that time. But Caroline was persistent and curious. If I didn't want to write about that, what did I want to write about?

I knew immediately: a book about how Black people gather around food to create safety, joy, and connection. And in doing so, I said, I thought we'd uncover some important lessons that could be applied to food justice movements. That is how we got here. That is how I got the opportunity to write a book about people and practices I love and beliefs that keep me buoyed through the roughest times.

As you've probably figured out from reading this book, gathering people is one of the greatest joys of my life. I love to cook. Like Aunt Helen in chapter 2, I get a great deal of satisfaction from knowing that people love what I've prepared for them. If they're especially gracious, I'll promise to cook for them again. This seems like a small thing in a world with so many forms of inequity, but sometimes the smallest things are the sturdiest building blocks for the world we want to build. In this case, the smallest things—like cooking for friends, taking a dish to a repast, or hosting a cookout—help us cultivate dignity, joy, mutual recognition, and pleasure. I've spent a lot of time asking: how do we build our food movements around *those* things? *Gather* is one exploration of that question. I'm sure there will be many, many more.

I think about that ASA panel often. It's one of my favorite moments as an academic. Not because my presentation was so great. Not even because I managed to get a room full of people to dance in a hotel meeting hall. I think about it because, as clichéd as it may sound, it was a micro version of the world I desperately want to live in. In our session abstract, we promised that our session would be "an occasion to share sustenance, groove together, imbibe the spirit, stoke joy, nurse grief, make space, and spread some love in public. Come through." We fulfilled that promise; and because we did, this book was made possible. If I have any hope for what you will do after reading *Gather*, it is that you accept invitations to be with others—in love, in joy, in grief, in rage-—and that you submit to being transformed in the process. It is through our individual and communal transformations that the world is changed. Or, in the beautiful words of science fiction writer Octavia E. Butler, "All that you touch you Change. All that you Change Changes you. The only lasting truth is Change. God is Change."

At home in Austin, I share a garden with my dear friend Ashley. When we decided to start our garden, we researched the best methods for constructing raised beds and what would grow well in the Texas climate. When we got around to implementing them, we struggled. We didn't have enough hands or tools. We cursed the day we'd decided to become gardeners in the wretched Texas heat and had to acknowledge that our ambition outpaced our skills. But we kept going, learning as much as we could about cruelty-free insect repellents and how to keep our tomatoes from burning up in the sun. At the end of our first season, we were pretty proud of ourselves, having sustained a thriving herb garden, grown two watermelons, and produced a modest amount of okra. I told y'all I hate okra, but I grew it for the culture!

We did not begin our garden because we want to be master growers. We started it because Ashley, as a historian of the Black power movement, and I, as a food studies scholar, both believe deeply in one thing: Black people cannot afford to be hyper-individualistic. Across Black history, communalism is the one value that, I believe, has sustained us from enslavement until now, when assaults on Black life range from food apartheid to housing inequities to over-policing. Black people return to communalism over and over again in the spirit of Sankofa, the Twi word that means "to return" or to "go back and get it."

Our garden, our shared responsibility, has been a lesson in grace (sometimes we drop the ball); flexibility (sometimes we need to work around the other's schedule); work (who's going to pull the weeds?); accountability (let's not leave each other hanging); and shared joy (I have never seen two people more excited about watermelon). Our garden is not at a scale that can feed communities. That is not our goal. But our garden, like that at Pleasant Hope, like others across the country, is a practice space where we get to work out what nourishment means for and with each other. That nourishment has to do with what we grow, but it is also a pocket of hope, joy, and connection. To borrow the words of a gardener I met in D.C. while researching my first book, the garden is a symbol that we will keep flourishing.

There is an art to gathering that is rooted in collective nourishment. That art can be cultivated, but it requires us to embrace creativity, risk, and communalism. Gathering doesn't require perfection. If it did, Heber Brown would have given up on gardening at the first sign of criticism and skepticism from his congregation. If it did, the Cockrill and Johnson family reunions would not have happened once it was clear that costs were too much and hands on deck were too few. If it did, Chef Tam's vision for a repast for Tyre Nichols's family would not have gotten off the ground once she realized how many people would need to be fed. If it did, Austin's mutual aid collectives would have failed as soon as we saw empty shelves at grocery stores during Winter Storm Uri or as soon as the police arrived on the UT–Austin campus. What gathering *does* require is a willingness to build something that may not be easily measurable or standardized.

Our consumption choices are complex, messy, sometimes healthy, sometimes not. But more importantly, our consumption choices reflect much more than meeting biological needs. They tell stories about what we have access to, who is important to us, our cultural heritage, and what foods embody celebration or mourning. This is where I believe we can grow our food justice movements: to broaden our understanding and metrics such that we take into account both our biological needs and our cultural and communal ones. In other words, we need more frameworks for understanding nourishment beyond what food is and isn't available.

In fact, perhaps the beauty of gathering as I've explored it here is the diverse ways it happens. From Chef Tam organizing other restaurant owners to put together a repast for Tyre Nichols's family to the sometimes exhausting labor of planning a family reunion, what each gathering in this book teaches us is that there's something important about meeting *specific* needs in *specific* moments, even if we are drawing from deeply loved traditions. The diversity of styles, approaches, and outcomes isn't a weakness. It is a strength. Nourishment is more than meeting caloric needs; it's also about feeding the social body. Nourishment can provide a holistic framework that enables people to live their very best lives.

When faced with challenges or unexpected outcomes, we all have an impulse to do something. Sometimes that impulse leads us out into the streets, as in the summer of 2020 when every state in the US had at least one protest in the wake of the deaths of Breonna Taylor and George Floyd. Sometimes that impulse leads us to serve at repasts or to gather our families for a reunion after a pandemic has wreaked havoc. Sometimes it leads us to organize a group of colleagues and strangers to provide mutual aid during a natural disaster. That impulse, the one that leads us toward people instead of away from them, is the impulse to gather. It is the simple, fundamental human need to be together. In these moments, it is not caloric intake we're worried about, but the work of nourishing the soul.

The moment we're in is all that we're ever guaranteed, so we must make the most of it. Perhaps the moment we choose to nourish one another is all we really have. By doing so, we can change the conditions we live in and the conditions for seven generations to come. When I stepped into the role of sacred gatherer, I did so in the lineage of women and communities that had already paved a way. Now, I am (as are so many of you!) paving new pathways for people who will inhabit this Earth long after we're gone. Maybe some of the seeds we plant today won't sprout for years to come, depending on the environment they've been sown into. Justice, as a practice and a concept, is ephemeral, meaning it is not set in stone. Like seasons and gardens, it's always changing, and something is always growing, ready to be tended.

I didn't know when I was growing up that early lessons in food, nourishment, and care would pave the way for my future career. To be honest, I didn't even immediately make the connection between the lessons from my grandmother's kitchen and my study of food justice when I decided to become an anthropologist. But I always knew that gathering was integral to our way of life. From Juneteenth celebrations to church homecomings to picking plums and peaches for elderly family members who were also our neighbors, most of my formative years were spent learning how to *be* with people and what preparing, distributing, and consuming food meant in that process. Now, I consider it a privilege that, as an anthropologist, I get to spend time learning with and from others about what makes them feel nourished, whole, and alive. Doing this work is one of the greatest joys of my life. It is work that I believe has the power to transform our food systems and our world writ large. It may not be your life's work, but I hope the stories in this book at least help you think about what you practice at an everyday scale and how those practices can point us either toward or away from a more equitable world.

Dear reader, I opened *Gather* with an invitation. I invited you to be curious, hopeful, and a bit skeptical about what gardens, reunions, repasts, and mutual aid have to do with food justice. I was asking you to suspend judgment—especially concerning stereotypes you might have learned about Black people and food—and to stretch your imagination about what's possible. After witnessing the many ways that people stretch their capacity to form a "we" with one another, serve one another, create safety with and for one another, and practice ancestral reverence and remembrance with one another, I wonder: What have you learned about transformation? Where do you see yourself in the collective "we" in our pursuit of a more just society? I've left much for you to ponder—more questions than answers. Exactly as it should be, to keep the gathering going.

ACKNOWLEDGMENTS

People often say that writing a book can be a lonely endeavor, but you're never doing it alone. That feels very true to me. While I wrestled with ideas and words on the page, there were many people who cheered me on, offered feedback, brought me dinner, or generally shared their excitement about this book until I too couldn't help but remain excited. Some of those people are part of the editorial dream team that saw *Gather*'s potential from the beginning. Sarah Levitt, my Capricorn kindred and agent: Thank you for helping me dream bigger and be more confident in my ideas, and for translating industry-speak into language I understand. To my phenomenal editors, Caroline Adams and Michael Moss: The gap between academic publishing and trade publishing can feel wide and confusing, but I can honestly say that you two made the transition feel effortless. Thank you for your thoughtful editorial feedback and unwavering support. As I was nearing the submission deadline, I found myself overwhelmed with details—like *What do you mean I have to turn footnotes into narrative notes?!* To Kristin Thiel: You stepped in and saved the day. Thank you for your attention to details and for your little notes of encouragement throughout the revision phases. To Allegra

Huston: Thank you for your generosity during the copyediting phase. You didn't have to leave positive notes along the way, but you did ... and they kept me encouraged when I was tired of rereading my own words. To Maggie Dickinson, Hanna Garth, and Stephen Satterfield: Thank you for being in conversation with me, reading things at the midnight hour. Your work has inspired me. *Gather* is possible because of your dynamic thinking. And to Khari Johnson, my research assistant: You are the definition of shoot your shot! I am so grateful that you reached out to me on Twitter when you first heard of this project. You're not only a fantastic research assistant, you're also a beautiful thinker. I can't wait to see the book(s) you'll write about Black people and food in the future!

Few people will know what it took for me to write this book in the period of my life when it was written. Even I am amazed that I did. It is literally a product of being gathered in love by friends who really understood what I needed to get this book done. They have been my closest companions, cheerleaders, and the people who grounded me when much of the world felt unstable and uncertain. There will never be enough words to thank them all for the soul-nourishing care they offered, but I want to try. To my family: You have always given me space to do exactly what I wanted to do in this world, and I am grateful for it. It may have taken a while to integrate the lessons from Cooper Settlement into my life and research, but I am here now. Thank you for witnessing. To Savannah Shange: Sometimes I feel unworthy of how much you hype me up, but you have consistently believed in me as a writer and a human. Your presence in my life makes me sit up a little taller. Somehow, we've gone from near-strangers to chosen family, and I am a happier, healthier human because of that intentionality and care. When I am with you (in spirit or in the flesh), I feel held. To Ashley Farmer: I'm so glad people get to meet you in the pages of this book. I hope they see even a glimpse of who I know you to be—someone who is kind, supportive, and down to take risks. It isn't an exaggeration to say that meeting you in 2020 changed my life for the better. You (and Ella!) have pulled me through some rough times, and I'm incredibly grateful. You may hate to talk about feelings, but I hope that in the absence of words, my love and gratitude are deeply felt. To Tommi (and Roscoe the Recalcitrant Pug): You have been an amazing cheerleader. Thank you for accompanying me to talks, for reading drafts when I needed to see how my words landed for people outside my field, and for all the care work you did along the way to make sure I could do my best work in the world. The behind-the-scenes domestic labor done by others doesn't always get the shout-out it deserves. I want you to know that every single thing you did to create a home contributed to this book, and I am grateful for it. Bianca Williams, Amira Rose Davis, Chelsi West Ohueri: Thank you for the writing accountability, for reading drafts, and for being co-thinkers along the way. The way each of you models Black feminist community-building and care inspires me. Loron Benton, Dara Cooper, Renée Skeete, Solana Shaw, Bridget McLennon, and Leigh Syphax: Being your friend is a constant reminder of what it means to be seen by others over a long arc of time. You've been on this journey with me for a while now, seen me through several transitions, and you've never wavered in support. Thank you for being part of my home base. And to Nadine Mattis, the *ultimate* gatherer: I am so grateful for you and the space you co-curate at Easton's Nook. It is the epitome of what gathering means and can do in the world. Thank you for your meals and your listening ear, and for making oxtail when I ask! Reader, whenever I say Black women always save my life, these women are exactly who I mean.

To Karma Chavez: You inspire me. I respect your leadership, your activism, and your commitment to being a good, kind human. When I was writing the mutual aid chapter, you were the reader in my mind, because you hold me and so many others accountable for showing up for others. Thank you for your friendship, and for letting me into your bunker if the apocalypse comes. I promise to not show up empty handed! To the Turn Up Crew: It was love at first magic show. Thank you all for wrapping me in your love, for letting me love your babies, and for always being down to gather together. Being part of you has changed my entire sense of what it is possible to build with colleagues-turned-friends. To the people who follow my journey on Facebook and Instagram: Thank you for eagerly providing song recommendations and anecdotes of your own experiences with gatherings. To my colleagues at UT–Austin, especially Cherise Smith and Simone Brown: Both of you provided tangible support and encouragement (and walks!) during this writing process. Thank you for sharing your wisdom with me.

Lastly and most importantly, thank you to every single person who submitted a story, sat for an interview, or invited me to come to your family reunion. I was humbled by the outpouring of interest, and I hope I've represented the essence of who you are and how you gather well. This book is because of you, and it is for you. I really hope you're proud.

GATHER: A PLAYLIST

While I was writing *Gather*, I put out a call on social media asking people to share songs they associate with Black gatherings. Some songs were suggested over and over (e.g., "Family Reunion," "Before I Let Go," and almost all the line-dancing songs). This playlist is based on those suggestions. Though I didn't include every song, I tried to preserve the vibe: mostly fun, lighthearted bops that encourage full-body joy. Not all the songs here are kid-appropriate or appropriate for all situations (most people wouldn't play "Back That Azz Up" in a church garden, for example), so I encourage you to further curate it according to your needs and personalize it for your own gatherings. What songs would you add?

"24K Magic" (Bruno Mars)
"ABC" (The Jackson 5)
"As" (Stevie Wonder)
"Back That Azz Up" (Juvenile, Lil' Wayne, and Mannie Fresh)
"Before I Let Go" (Maze and Frankie Beverly)
"Before I Let Go—Homecoming Live" (Beyoncé)
"Blow the Whistle" (Too $hort)
"Bunny Hop" (Da Entourage)
"Candy" (Cameo)
"Cha Cha Slide" (DJ Casper)
"Church Girl" (Beyoncé)

"Cupid Shuffle" (Cupid)
"Don't Think I'm Not" (Kandi)
"Down Home Blues" (Z. Z. Hill)
"Electric Slide" (Grandmaster Slice)
"Everybody Loves the Sunshine" (Roy Ayers)
"Family Reunion" (The O'Jays)
"Feels Good" (Tony! Toni! Toné!)
"Freedom" (Jon Batiste)
"Hey Mr. D.J." (Zhané)
"Hot in Herre" (Nelly)
"I'm So into You" (SWV)
"Joy & Pain" (Maze and Frankie Beverly)
"Just Fine" (Mary J. Blige)
"Just Got Paid" (Johnny Kemp)
"Knuck if You Buck" (Crime Mob, Lil Scrappy)
"Last Two Dollars" (Johnnie Taylor)
"Livin' for the Weekend" (The O'Jays)
"Love and Happiness" (Al Green)
"Love Is the Message" (MFSB, The Three Degrees)
"Lovely Day" (Bill Withers)
"Love on Top" (Beyoncé)
"Milkshake" (Kelis)
"Motownphilly" (Boyz II Men)
"My Boo" (Ghost Town DJs)
"MY HOUSE" (Beyoncé)
"Never Too Much" (Luther Vandross)
"Night to Remember" (Shalamar)
"Outstanding" (The Gap Band)
"People Everyday" (Arrested Development)
"Rapper's Delight" (The Sugarhill Gang)
"Return of the Mack" (Mark Morrison)
"September" (Earth, Wind, & Fire)
"Signed, Sealed, Delivered" (Stevie Wonder)
"Summertime" (DJ Jazzy Jeff & The Fresh Prince)
"This Is How We Do It" (Montell Jordan)
"We Are One" (Maze and Frankie Beverly)
"Wobble" (V.I.C.)
"Work It" (Missy Elliott)

NOTES

INTRODUCTION: WHY GATHER?

2 **truly disadvantaged**: W. J. Wilson, *The Truly Disadvantaged: The Inner City, the Underclass, and Public Policy* (University of Chicago Press, 2012).
4 **"nourish"**: These definitions were taken from the online Oxford English Dictionary.
6 **least access to fresh, healthy food**: Winkler et al.'s study was cited in "Poor and Black-Majority Neighborhoods of Atlanta Lack Access to Fresh Produce, Study Finds," written by Rob DiRienzo and published by FOX 5 Atlanta on September 21, 2023.
8 **the term "food apartheid"**: Anna Bronnes, "Karen Washington: It's Not a Food Desert, It's Food Apartheid," *Guernica*, May 7, 2018.
9 **Food justice has received**: Robert Gottlieb and Anupama Joshi, *Food Justice* (MIT Press, 2010), 6.
11 **construct justice and liberation in our food system**: "The Path Forward for Food and Ag: Leading Voices in the Food Movement Respond to a Second Trump Administration, and Discuss Where We Go From Here," *Civil Eats*, November 13, 2024.
13 **Black aliveness**: Kevin Quashie opens *Black Aliveness, Or a Poetics of Being* (Duke University Press, 2021) with the following words: "What would it mean to consider black aliveness, especially given how readily—and literally—blackness is indexed to death? To behold such aliveness, we have to imagine a black world . . . we have to imagine a black world so as to surpass the everywhere and everyway of black death, of blackness that is understood only through such a vocabulary. This equation of blackness

and death is indisputable and enduring, surely, but if we want to try to conceptualize aliveness, we have to begin somewhere else."

15 **care that recognizes the shared risks and rewards**: Christina Sharpe offered the notion of "care as shared risk" in *In the Wake: On Blackness and Being* (Duke University Press, 2016).

15 **anthropologist Hanna Garth**: Hanna Garth, *Food in Cuba: The Pursuit of a Decent Meal* (Stanford University Press, 2020), 5.

17 **"For where two or three gather in my name"**: Matthew 18:20 (New International Version).

CHAPTER 1: GARDENS

19 **nearly half of the churches and other faith-based organizations**: Brad R. Fulton, "Nearly Half of All Churches and Other Faith Institutions Help People Get Enough to Eat," *The Conversation*, October 28, 2021. This article includes data from the National Congregations Study.

23 **one in five people in Baltimore**: Johns Hopkins Center for a Livable Future and Baltimore City's Office of Sustainability, "New, Improved 'Food Desert' Map," March 5, 2012.

23 **The USDA Food Access Research Atlas**: This tool allows you to see food access indicators for census tracts across the United States. With it, you can see if an area has low access (measured by the distance to a supermarket), is low-income, or has limited access to cars. It is a great tool for exploring your own neighborhood or areas you frequent.

24 **"the land remained the Earth"**: Sylvia Wynter, "Novel and History, Plot and Plantation," *Savacou* 5 (June 1971): 99.

25 **braided okra seeds into their hair**: Leah Penniman, "Black to the Land," in *We Are Each Other's Harvest: Celebrating African American Farmers, Land, and Legacy*, edited by Natalie Baszile (HarperCollins, 2021), 61.

26 **Vernon Johns**: For an in-depth exploration of Vernon Johns's life and activism, check out William J. Mackie and Patrick L. Cooney, *Vernon Johns: "It's Safe to Murder Negroes"* (published by authors, 2016).

26 **growing food could unite rural and urban**: "A Negro Agrarian," *Opportunity: A Journal of Negro Life* 40, no. 11 (1933): 336.

26 **"sick and tired of being sick and tired"**: Fannie Lou Hamer said these words in a speech delivered on December 20, 1964, at Williams Institutional CME Church in Harlem, New York. The speech was in support of the Mississippi Freedom Democratic Party.

27 **Greenwood Food Blockade**: For two great histories of the Greenwood

Food Blockade, the general food conditions of the time, and various forms of resistance, see Monica M. White's *Freedom Farmers: Agricultural Resistance and the Black Freedom Movement* (University of North Carolina Press, 2019) and Bobby Smith II's *Food Power Politics: The Food Story of the Mississippi Civil Rights Movement* (University of North Carolina Press, 2023).

27 **emancipatory food power**: Smith, *Food Power Politics*, 2.

27 **"Down where we are"**: White, *Freedom Farmers*, 65.

28 **"Anyone who has two shirts"**: Luke 3:11 (New International Version).

31 **systemic efforts to thwart their land ownership**: Leah Penniman, *Farming While Black: Soul Fire Farm's Practical Guide to Liberation on the Land* (Chelsea Green Publishing, 2018), 350–56; Kali Holloway, "How Thousands of Black Farmers Were Forced Off Their Land," *The Nation*, November 1, 2021.

32 **that number had decreased to 3,595**: E. Demissie, "A History of Black Farm Operators in Maryland," *Agriculture and Human Values* 9, no. 1 (1992): 24.

32 **city-owned vacant lots**: For a more comprehensive exploration of how community gardens start on city-owned plots, consult Kristin Reynolds and Nevin Cohen, *Beyond the Kale: Urban Agriculture and Social Justice Activism in New York City*, vol. 28 of Geographies of Justice and Social Transformation, edited by Nik Heynen, Mathew Coleman, and Spana Doshi (University of Georgia Press, 2016).

37 **"There is no excuse"**: Eric Garland, "WATCH: Obama's Full Remarks on Baltimore," *The Hill*, April 28, 2015.

37 **"language of the unheard"**: From a speech titled "The Other America," given by Martin Luther King Jr. in 1967. Video of this speech, as well as its transcript (quote is at para. 29), is available through the Civil Rights Movement Archive.

37 **84 percent of Baltimore students**: Evie Blad, "Amid Baltimore Turmoil, Students and Educators Seek Understanding," *EducationWeek*, May 1, 2015.

37 **an article that connected**: Richard A. Oppel Jr., "West Baltimore's Police Presence Drops, and Murders Soar," *New York Times*, June 12, 2015.

38 **"When city services backed up"**: Kendall Vanderslice, "Reverend Dr. Heber Brown and the Black Church Food Security Network," *Good Food Jobs*, October 9, 2018, para 12.

39 **Black churches have built housing units**: Nadia Mian, "Black Con-

gregations Are Developing Housing on Church Land," *Shelterforce*, January 17, 2023.

41 **five loaves of bread and two fish**: In the New International Version of the Bible, Matthew 14:13–21, Mark 6:31–44, Luke 9:10–17, and John 6:1–14 all tell a variation of the story of Jesus feeding a crowd of over five thousand with five loaves of bread and two fish.

42 **making a wayward life**: Saidiya Hartman, *Wayward Lives, Beautiful Experiments: Intimate Histories of Riotous Black Girls, Troublesome Women, and Queer Radicals* (W. W. Norton, 2019).

42 **"Sit. Feast on your life"**: Derek Walcott, "Love After Love," in *Collected Poems 1948–1984* (Farrar, Straus and Giroux, 1986).

CHAPTER 2: REUNIONS

45 **worst air quality in the world**: The Air Quality Index was between 425 and 500 at its worst, well over the lowest "hazardous" level of 300. "Philadelphia Now Has Worst Air Quality Compared to All Major Cities," *CBS News Philadelphia*, June 7, 2023.

50 **"too sophisticated to dig in the ground"**: Ashanté M. Reese, *Black Food Geographies: Race, Self-Reliance, and Food Access in Washington, D.C.* (University of North Carolina Press, 2019), 81.

51 **133 billion pounds of food**: "Why Should We Care About Food Waste?," USDA.gov, accessed March 19, 2025.

51 **"ugly" fruits and vegetables**: "Fighting Food Waste and Hunger Through Food Rescue," Feeding America, accessed March 19, 2025.

51 **a charity model and a justice model**: Jan Poppendieck, "Dilemmas of Emergency Food: A Guide for the Perplexed," *Agriculture and Human Values* 11 (1994): 69.

52 **50 million people**: "Charitable Food Assistance Participation," Feeding America, November 12, 2024.

54 **soul food**: For robust histories and discussions of soul food, see Adrian Miller's *Soul Food: The Surprising Story of an American Cuisine* (University of North Carolina Press, 2013) and Jennifer Jensen Wallach's *Dethroning the Deceitful Pork Chop: Rethinking African American Foodways from Slavery to Obama* (University of Arkansas Press, 2015)

54 **vibe of Black gatherings and spaces**: Kaily Heitz, "Feeling the Vibe: Relations and Praxes of a Black Sense of Place in Oakland, California," *Antipode*, March 18, 2024.

54 **"Black food energy"**: Psyche A. Williams-Forson, *Eating While Black:*

Food Shaming and Race in America (University of North Carolina Press, 2022), 156.

60 **"Where life is precious, life is precious"**: This is a phrase that Ruth Wilson Gilmore says often as a way to emphasize that a society that believes every life is valuable would create institutions and practices that reflect that. See Rachel Kushner, "Is Prison Necessary? Ruth Wilson Gilmore Might Change Your Mind," *New York Times Magazine*, April 17, 2019. To listen to Gilmore discuss the concept in the context of her abolitionist values, see an episode of the podcast *On Being* with the same title, published March 30, 2023.

62 ***Let the Circle Be Unbroken***: Mildred D. Taylor, *Let the Circle Be Unbroken* (Dial Press, 1981).

63 **reuniting with lost family members was a priority**: Heather Andrea Williams, *Help Me to Find My People: The African American Search for Family Lost in Slavery* (University of North Carolina Press, 2012), 1.

63 **Matt Terry**: "Matt Terry Searching for His Mother Harriet Wood (formerly Harriet Terry)," *Southern Christian Advocate* (New Orleans, LA), July 21, 1881, found on Last Seen: Finding Family After Slavery, accessed March 20, 2025.

64 **Eliza Jones**: "Eliza Jones Searching for Her Uncle Sam Roberson," *Houston Daily Post*, February 24, 1898, found on Last Seen: Finding Family After Slavery, accessed March 20, 2025. The full text of the advertisement reads: "Omen, Smith County, Texas, February 19.---Information wanted of my uncle, Sam Roberson; he is my father's brother. His father's name was Moses Roberson. The last I heard of him he lived close to Crockett, Houston county. Any information of his whereabouts will be thankfully received. Mrs. Eliza Jones, Omen, Smith County, Texas."

64 **Sam Grant**: "Sam Grant Searching for His Siblings Including Brother Oscar and Sister Betsy," *Southern Christian Advocate* (New Orleans, LA), August 17, 1882, found on Last Seen: Finding Family After Slavery, accessed March 20, 2025. The full text of the advertisement reads: "DEAR EDITOR: I wish to inquire for my kin people whom I left in Franklin County, Tennessee. I was brought to Texas in the winter of 1854, and left mother, two brothers, and a sister in Tennessee. In the spring of 1857 mother died. Her name was Martha, and she belonged to Elijah B. Rakin; my oldest brother Oscar belonged to John Miller, the next, Moses to Hayden March; the youngest, William to Jefferson Moore. Sister Betsy belonged to John Hiter, and was brought to Crockett,

Texas when I was ten years old. Sister Rose was sold out to the Moore family, and was carried to Memphis and I heard that she was living in Limestone county, Miss. The youngest was Mary Jane Ragan. Address me at Hallettsville, Texas. Sam Grant."

64 **Jiles Hunley**: "Jiles Hunley Searching for His Unnamed Mother, Sister Martha Jane, and brother George Hunley," *Southern Christian Advocate* (New Orleans, LA), March 3, 1881, found on Last Seen: Finding Family After Slavery, accessed March 20, 2025. The ad's text reads: "MR. EDITOR – I wish to inquire, through your valuable paper, for my relatives, viz: Mother, sister and brother. My mother belonged to Betsy Anderson, who married a man by the name of Minor Smith. I left her about thirty years ago for Texas. My sister's name was Martha Jane, she belonged to the widow Jennings who, I heard, died shortly after I left. I was brought to Texas by David Nealy and have not heard from either since I left them. They were both then living not far from DeKalb, Kemper county, Miss. Mother with the widow Smith, and sister with the widow Jennings. My brother's name was George Hunley, his wife's name was Mimy Hunley; he was taken from Mississippi by Dr. Hunley and Judget Marshall. Also my wife desires to know the whereabouts of her sons John and Madison. She left them with Jim Harrold, near Macklemoseville, Tenn, some time before the war; she was brought to Texas by Robert Barbee, after a stay of one year in Texas was returned to Tennessee, remained there one year, then brought to Texas again; have not seen her children since she left Tennessee second time, her name was then Penny Barbee. Any information relative to the above named relatives will be very thankfully appreciated. JILES HUNLEY. Crockett, Houston county, Texas."

67 **homeplace**: bell hooks used the word *homeplace* to mean "a site of resistance," in *Yearning: Race, Gender, and Cultural Politics* (South End Press, 1990), 41–49.

67 **all-encompassing weather**: "In my text, the weather is the totality of our environments; the weather is the total climate; and that climate is antiblack." Christina Sharpe, *In the Wake: On Blackness and Being* (Duke University Press, 2016), 104.

68 **the same kind of public spaces**: Here, I am referencing three high-profile examples of public spaces being unsafe for Black people: (a) Twelve-year-old Tamir Rice was shot and killed by a white police officer in Cleveland, Ohio, in 2014, when a police officer assumed the toy gun he was carrying was real. (b) "BBQ Becky" was the nickname given to Jennifer

Schulte in 2018 after she called 911 to report two Black men who were grilling in Lake Merritt, a park in gentrifying Oakland. In a second call, she reported that she was afraid after the dispatcher questioned why she felt threatened by a cookout. (c) In 2020, a white woman falsely accused Christian Cooper, a Black man who was in New York City's Central Park participating in his bird-watching hobby, of threatening her.

68 **public squares in the US**: Historically, public squares were used for slave auctions and public beatings. For an in-depth historical analysis of slave auctions in the US, see Anne C. Bailey, *The Weeping Time: Memory and the Largest Slave Auction in American History* (Cambridge University Press, 2017). For a gendered and spatial analysis of auction blocks, see Katherine McKittrick, *Demonic Grounds: Black Women and the Cartography of Struggle* (University of Minnesota Press, 2006).

69 **commensality**: Alice P. Julier, *Eating Together: Food, Friendship and Inequality* (University of Illinois Press, 2013), 4.

70 **"the 'itis"**: A colloquial term Black folks use to refer to a feeling of being full and sleepy. The technical term for this is *postprandial somnolence*.

CHAPTER 3: REPASTS

72 **"ordinary notes of care"**: Christina Sharpe, *Ordinary Notes* (Alfred A. Knopf Canada, 2023).

76 **grief in sartorial form**: Robin Brooks, "RIP shirts or shirts of the movement: Reading the death paraphernalia of Black lives," *Biography* 41, no. 4 (2018): 807–30.

78 **"a precondition of being together"**: Jennifer C. Nash, *How We Write Now: Living with Black Feminist Theory* (Duke University Press, 2024), 65.

78 **"Food knows all languages"**: Michael Lee West, *Consuming Passions: A Food-Obsessed Life* (HarperCollins, 2000), 139.

78 **"food for the bereaved"**: West, *Consuming Passions*, 132.

79 **"it is just the Christian thing to do"**: Joshua Graham, "Funeral Food as Resurrection in the American South," in *Dying to Eat: Cross-Cultural Perspectives on Food, Death, and the Afterlife*, edited by Candi K. Cann (University Press of Kentucky, 2018), 96.

79 **Christian concepts of mortality, memory, and the afterlife**: Benjamin M. Stewart, "Food and Funerals: Why Meals Matter for Christian Mortality and How We Might Respond Gustatorily to Changing Death Practices," *Liturgy* 32, no. 2 (2017): 52–61; David E. Sutton, *Remembrance of Repasts* (Bloomsbury Publishing, 2001).

79 **Kandiga, a community in northeast Ghana**: Victoria Mensah Nyamadi, Moses Nsoh Aberinga, and Russell Franklin Nyamadi, "Traditional funeral rites: A useful ancient tradition or a threat to our food security? A case of the Kandiga community of Ghana," *International Journal of Academic Research in Business and Social Sciences* 5, no. 11 (2015): 312–22.

79 **Mala Batha**: Annie Hariharan, Communing with Spirits and Coping with Death: Grief Food in Three Cultures," Al Jazeera, March 30, 2024.

80 **"Bringing store-bought food"**: Karla FC Holloway, *Passed On: African American Mourning Stories, a Memorial* (Duke University Press, 2020), 166.

80 **"Against the back wall"**: Haile Eshe Cole, "The Repast: Self and Collective Love in the Face of Black Death," *Women, Gender, and Families of Color* 7, no. 2 (2019): 204.

81 **"Weeping may endure for a night"**: Psalm 30:5 (New International Version).

83 **"the hunger capital of the US"**: The report was cited in Jamel Major, "Study Names Memphis 'Hunger Capital of the United States,'" published by *Action News 5* on March 29, 2010.

83 **22.5 percent of Memphians live below the poverty line**: This figure was reported in the Memphis Poverty Fact Sheet, which is compiled annually by Dr. Elena Delavega of the University of Memphis and data consultant Dr. Gregory M. Blumenthal.

84 **underlying mechanisms that fuel this conundrum**: Alison G. M. Brown, Layla E. Esposito, Rachel A. Fisher, Holly L. Nicastro, Derrick C. Tabor, and Jenelle R. Walker, "Food Insecurity and Obesity: Research Gaps, Opportunities, and Challenges," *Translational Behavioral Medicine* 9, no. 5 (2019): 980–87.

84 **"a failing of basic humanity"**: Isabelle McDonnell, Megan Myers, and Jon Michael Raasch, "Memphis Businesses Board Up in Preparation for Release of Tyre Nichols Bodycam Video," Fox News, January 27, 2023.

CHAPTER 4: MUTUAL AID

92 **natural gas company boasted about the revenue**: Charean Williams, "Texas Freeze Allows Jerry Jones' Natural Gas Company to 'Hit Jackpot,'" *Pro Football Talk*, February 17, 2021.

96 **Anarchist philosopher Peter Kropotkin**: Peter Kropotkin, *Mutual Aid: A Factor in Evolution* (1902; Extending Horizons Books, 1976), 125.

97 **Mutual aid is a powerful way to self-organize**: William C. Anderson, "Another Way Out: Self-Organize Now or Self-Organize Later," *Prism*, October 29, 2024.
97 **three key elements of mutual aid projects**: Dean Spade, *Mutual Aid: Building Solidarity During This Crisis (and the Next)* (Verso, 2020).
98 **"witnessing 2.0"**: Deborah A. Thomas, *Political Life in the Wake of the Plantation* (Duke University Press, 2019), 2–3.
99 **"How can we build the networks"**: Bench Ansfield, "Abolition Infrastructures: A Conversation on Transformative Justice with Rachel Herzing and Dean Spade," *Radical History Review* 147 (October 2023): 201.
101 **as students at Columbia**: Johanna Alonso, "More Than 100 Students Arrested at Columbia," *Inside Higher Ed*, April 18, 2024.
102 **ramifications of this ban**: Johanna Alonso, "'Heartbreaking to Be Collateral' in the Battle Over DEI," *Inside Higher Ed*, July 29, 2024.
108 **freedom is not only an idea**: Gilmore, *Abolition Geography* (Verso, 2022).
109 **"Rest is a form of resistance"**: Tricia Hersey, *Rest Is Resistance: A Manifesto* (Hachette, 2022), 16.

CONCLUSION: GATHERING ON THE BRINK OF UNCERTAINTY

114 **"All that you touch you Change"**: Octavia E. Butler, *Parable of the Sower* (Seven Stories Press, 1993), 3.

FURTHER READING

CHAPTER 1: GARDENS

Carter, Christopher. *The Spirit of Soul Food: Race, Faith, and Food Justice* (University of Illinois Press, 2021).

Dungy, Camille T. *Soil: The Story of a Black Mother's Garden* (Simon & Schuster, 2023).

Penniman, Leah. *Farming While Black: Soul Fire Farm's Practical Guide to Liberation on the Land* (Chelsea Green, 2018).

Reese, Ashanté M. *Black Food Geographies: Race, Self-Reliance, and Food Access in Washington, D.C.* (University of North Carolina Press, 2019).

Reynolds, Kristin, and Nevin Cohen. *Beyond the Kale: Urban Agriculture and Social Justice Activism in New York City* (University of Georgia Press, 2016).

Smith, Bobby J., II. *Food Power Politics: The Food Story of the Mississippi Civil Rights Movement* (University of North Carolina Press, 2023).

White, Monica M. *Freedom Farmers: Agricultural Resistance and the Black Freedom Movement* (University of North Carolina Press, 2018).

CHAPTER 2: REUNIONS

Miles, Tiya. *All That She Carried: The Journey of Ashley's Sack, a Black Family Keepsake* (Random House, 2022).

Smart-Grosvenor, Vertamae. *Vibration Cooking: Or, the Travel Notes of a Geechee Girl* (University of Georgia Press, 2011).

Williams, Heather Andrea. *Help Me to Find My People: The African American Search for Family Lost in Slavery* (University of North Carolina Press, 2012).

Williams-Forson, Psyche A. *Eating While Black: Food Shaming and Race in America* (University of North Carolina Press, 2022).

CHAPTER 3: REPASTS

Holloway, Karla FC. *Passed On: African American Mourning Stories, a Memorial* (Duke University Press, 2020).

Sharpe, Christina. *Ordinary Notes* (Knopf Canada, 2023).

Sutton, David E. *Remembrance of Repasts* (Bloomsbury, 2001).

CHAPTER 4: MUTUAL AID

Allard, Jenna, and Carl Davidson, eds. *Solidarity Economy: Building Alternatives for People and Planet* (ChangeMaker, 2010).

Anderson, William C., and Zoé Samudzi. *As Black as Resistance: Finding the Conditions for Liberation* (AK Press, 2018).

Kaba, Mariame. *We Do This 'Til We Free Us: Abolitionist Organizing and Transforming Justice* (Haymarket, 2021).

Kropotkin, Peter. *Mutual Aid: A Factor in Evolution* (1902; Extending Horizons, 1976).

Piepzna-Samarasinha, Leah Lakshmi, and Ejeris Dixon, eds. *Beyond Survival: Strategies and Stories from the Transformative Justice Movement* (AK Press, 2020).

Spade, Dean. *Mutual Aid: Building Solidarity During This Crisis (and the Next)* (Verso, 2020).

COOKBOOKS

Lewis, Edna. *In Pursuit of Flavor* (Knopf, 2020).

Magness, Perre. *The Southern Sympathy Cookbook: Funeral Food with a Twist* (Countryman Press, 2018).

National Council of Negro Women. *The Black Family Reunion Cookbook* (Simon & Schuster, 1991).

Taylor, Nicole A. *Watermelon & Red Birds: A Cookbook for Juneteenth and Black Celebrations* (Simon & Schuster, 2022).

FURTHER READING

Terry, Bryant. *Black Food* (Ten Speed Press, 2021).

Tipton-Martin, Toni. *Jubilee: Recipes from Two Centuries of African American Cooking* (Penguin Random House, 2019).

Tipton-Martin, Toni. *Juke Joints, Jazz Clubs and Juice: Cocktails from Two Centuries of African American Cookbooks* (Clarkson Potter, 2023).

Turshen, Julia. *Feed the Resistance: Recipes and Ideas for Getting Involved* (Chronicle, 2017).

INDEX

Page numbers beginning with 125 refer to notes.

16th Street Baptist Church, 30

Acre Restaurant, 86
Adams, Caroline, 113
Africa, 25
Afroecology, 12
aliveness, 13, 125–26
American Studies Association (ASA) conference, 112–13, 114
Ashley (friend), 94, 103–4, 114–15
Austin Justice Coalition (AJC), 95
autonomy, 24–25, 26, 42–43

Beauty Shop, 86
Bedour (friend), 93–94
Black aliveness, 13, 125–26
Black Aliveness (Quashie), 125–26
Black Church Food Security Network (BCFSN), 20, 38–40
Black food energy, 54–55
Black Mamas ATX, 95
Black Panther Party, 9, 30
Black Urban Growers (BUGs), 8, 20
Booker, Cory, 32
Brooks, Robin, 76

Brown, Heber, III, 19–23, 25–26, 28–36, 38–43
Buntin, James, 59
Butler, Octavia E., 73–74

calling in, 40
canning, 34
capitalism, 70, 97, 98–99, 109
change, 73–74
charity, 51, 52–53
Chassidy (Ebow family), 55–56
chow chow, 34
churches, 20, 38–40. *See also individual churches*
civil rights movement, 26–27
class, 26, 29
Cockrill family, 57–62, 65–66
Cocozza, 86
Cole, Haile Eshe, 80
collard greens, 47
collectivism, 97. *See also* mutual aid
Columbia University, 100–101
communalism, 115. *See also* mutual aid
Communities of Color United (CCU), 95
community (general), 16–17, 36

INDEX

Consuming Passions (West), 78
consumption choices, 116
"Cook Out: Blackness with No Roof" panel, 112–13, 114
Cooper, Christian, 131
Cooper, Dara, 71
Cooper Settlement, 67, 110
cooperation. *See* mutual aid
cooption, 10
Coretta Scott King Young Women's Leadership Academy, 6
Crystal (Johnson family reunion), 45–47, 68
cultural guerrilla resistance, 24–25

DEI positions, 102
Dexter Avenue Baptist Church, 26

Ebow family, 55–56
Ecco, 86
Emancipation, 63–65, 129–30
emancipatory food power, 27
emergency food provisioning, 52–53
encampments, 100–106, 109
English, Kelly, 86

family reunions (general), 53–54, 65, 66, 67–69, 70–71. *See also* Cockrill family; Ebow family; Johnson family
family-history tours, 55–57
farming, 26. *See also* gardens
Federal Surplus Food Commodity Program, 27
Floyd, George, 117
food apartheid, 7–8
food energy, 54–55
food inequity, 6–8. *See also* food justice; food security; poverty
food justice, 9–10, 12, 51, 52–53. *See also* food inequity; food security
Food Justice (Gottlieb and Joshi), 9

Food Recovery Network, 51
food security, 22–23, 51. *See also* food justice
food system, 96
food waste, 51
Free Breakfast for Children, 9
Freedom Farms Cooperative, 27–28
funerals. *See* repasts

gardens
  Ashley and Ashanté's, 114–15
  during enslavement, 23–24
  Freedom Farms Cooperative, 27–28
  Johns' ideas, 26
  Pleasant Hope Baptist church, 21, 25–26, 29–30, 31–36, 38–43
  as threat, 30–31
  in vacant lots, 32
Garth, Hanna, 15
gender, 33
Ghana, 79
Gillibrand, Kirsten, 32
Gilmore, Ruth Wilson, 129
giardiniera, 34
Graham, Joshua, 78–79
Granger, Bagwell and Minerva, 24
Grant, Sam, 64, 129
Gray, Freddie, 36–38
Green Scheme, 9
Greenwood Food Blockade, 27
grief, 81, 82
guerrilla resistance, 24–25

Hamer, Fannie Lou, 9, 21, 26–28, 126
Hartman, Saidiya, 42
Hartzell, Jay, 102
health, 7, 84
healthy food, 6, 7–8, 53, 54. *See also* food justice
Heitz, Kaily, 54
Help Me to Find My People (Williams), 63

heroes, 108
Hersey, Tricia, 109
Holloway, Karla FC, 80
hospitality, 66
Hunley, Jiles, 64, 130

improvisation, 3
individualism, 96
industrialized food system, 11
"the 'itis," 70, 131

Jefferson, Thomas, 24
Johns, Vernon, 26
Johns Hopkins Center for Health Disparities Solutions, 7
Johnson family, 45–50, 68
Jones, Eliza, 64, 129
Joshi, Anupama, 9
joy, 81
Julier, Alice P., 69
Justice for Black Farmers Act, 32

Kropotkin, Peter, 96, 97

lack vs. improvisation, 3
land ownership, 31–32
Last Seen: Finding Family After Slavery archive, 63
LaToya's funeral and repast, 72–78, 81, 89
leftovers, 51
Let the Circle Be Unbroken (Taylor), 62–63
listening, 98
lost family, 63–65, 129–30

Mala Batha, 79
Mama (grandmother), 1–5
Maxine, Mama, 22, 31–36, 38–39
McEwen's, 86
Memphis, 83
Monz, L.A., 57–58, 59–62
Mother Emanuel AME Church, 30
Muddy's Bake Shop, 86

Murriel, Keith, 83
mutual aid
    about, 96, 97, 98–99
    Cooper Settlement, 110
    frustration and, 107–8
    heroes, 108
    marginality and, 107
    need and, 98–99
    Palestine, 100–101, 105–7, 109
    responsibility and, 51
    as spatial practice, 110–11
    suffering and, 99
    Winter Storm Uri, 94–95, 97–98, 99–100

Nap Ministry, 109
Nash, Jennifer, 78
National Black Food and Justice Alliance (NBFJA), 12, 51–52, 71
need, 89–90, 109–10
Nichols, Tyre, 82–88
nourishment
    Black food energy, 54–55
    community and, 16–17
    defined, 4, 5, 12
    food justice and, 12
    Pleasant Hope garden, 36

Obama, Barack, 37
obesity, 84
okra, 25
Oppel, Richard, 37–38
oral history, 13–14
ownership, 52

Palestine solidarity, 100–107, 109
Parable of the Sower (Butler), 73–74
Patterson, Tamra "Chef Tam," 85–87
pests, 33
pickles, 34
piklinz, 34
plantations, 23–24

INDEX

playlist, 123–24
Pleasant Hope Baptist church, 19–23, 25–26, 28–36, 38–43
police, 36–38, 100, 101–2, 103–5
political education, 29–30
politics of adequacy, 15–16
Poppendieck, Jan, 51
potato salad, 18
poverty, 23, 83–84
power outages, 91–93
protests
    Gray's death, 36–38, 85
    impulse and, 117
    rest and, 109
    student encampments, 100–106, 109
    as threat, 111
    See also mutual aid
public spaces, 68, 130–31

Quashie, Kevin, 125–26

racism, 16–17, 27, 68, 92. *See also* white supremacy
radical hospitality, 66
Rasheed (Cockrill family), 58, 62
Rendezvous, 86
repasts, 72–81, 85–90
rest, 109
Restaurant Iris, 86
returning, 75–76
Rice, Tamir, 130
riots, 37
RIP T-shirts, 76
rituals, 14–15, 57, 59, 62–63. *See also individual rituals*

satisfaction, 69–71
saviors, 97
scale, 11
Schulte, Jennifer, 130–31
Searcy, Josephine, 59, 60
The Second Line, 86

seeds, 25
segregation, 7, 49–50
Shafik, Minouche, 100
Sharpe, Christina, 72
slavery, 23–24. *See also* Emancipation
Smith, Bobby, II, 27
Soil to Sanctuary Market, 40
Southwest Atlanta Growers Cooperative (SWAG), 9
Spade, Dean, 97, 99
Sri Lanka, 79
stigmatization, 54
student encampments, 100–106, 109
Student Nonviolent Coordinating Committee (SNCC), 27
Sunrise, 86
supermarkets, 35–36, 51
Suzanne, Felicia, 86

Taylor, Breonna, 117
Taylor, Mildred D., 62–63
Terry, Matt, 63–64
Thomas, Deborah, 98
traditions, 54
Travonnie (Cockrill family), 57, 59, 60
trust, 36
Tsunami, 86
Tune, Mama, 56–57

"ugly" food, 51
Underground Café, 85–87
USDA Food Access Research Atlas, 126
UT–Austin, 101–6

vacant lots, 32
values, 5
vibes, 54–55

wages, 52
Warren, Elizabeth, 32
Washington, Karen, 8

waste, 51
wayward lives, 42
Wells, RowVaughn, 85
West, Michael Lee, 78
white supremacy, 23, 27, 30, 40, 109. *See also* racism

Williams, Darryl, 83
Williams-Forson, Psyche, 54–55
Winkler, Megan, 6
Winter Storm Uri, 91–94, 97–98, 99–100
witnessing 2.0, 98
Wynter, Sylvia, 24–25

Norton Shorts

BRILLIANCE WITH BREVITY

W. W. Norton & Company has been independent since 1923, when William Warder Norton and Mary (Polly) D. Herter Norton first published lectures delivered at the People's Institute, the adult education division of New York City's Cooper Union. In the 1950s, Polly Norton transferred control of the company to its employees.

One hundred years after its founding, W. W. Norton & Company inaugurates a new century of visionary independent publishing with Norton Shorts. Written by leading-edge scholars, these eye-opening books deliver bold thinking and fresh perspectives in under two hundred pages.

Available Winter 2026

The Racial Wealth Gap: A Brief History by Mehrsa Baradaran

Imagination: A Manifesto by Ruha Benjamin

What's Real About Race?: Untangling Science, Genetics, and Society by Rina Bliss

Offshore: Stealth Wealth and the New Colonialism by Brooke Harrington

Sex Beyond "Yes": Pleasure and Agency for Everyone by Quill R Kukla

Fewer Rules, Better People: The Case for Discretion by Barry Lam

Explorers: A New History by Matthew Lockwood

Wild Girls: How the Outdoors Shaped the Women Who Challenged a Nation by Tiya Miles

The Trafficker Next Door: How Household Employers Exploit Domestic Workers by Rhacel Salazar Parreñas

Gather: Black Food, Nourishment, and the Art of Togetherness by Ashanté M. Reese

The Moral Circle: Who Matters, What Matters, and Why by Jeff Sebo

Against Technoableism: Rethinking Who Needs Improvement by Ashley Shew

Fear Less: Poetry in Perilous Times by Tracy K. Smith

Literary Theory for Robots: How Computers Learned to Write by Dennis Yi Tenen

Forthcoming

Merlin Chowkwanyun on the social determinants of health

Daniel Aldana Cohen on eco-apartheid

Jim Downs on cultural healing

Reginald K. Ellis on Black education versus Black freedom

Nicole Eustace on settler colonialism

Agustín Fuentes on human nature

Justene Hill Edwards on the history of inequality in America

Destin Jenkins on a short history of debt

Natalia Molina on the myth of assimilation

Tony Perry on water in African American culture and history

Beth Piatote on living with history

Daniel Steinmetz-Jenkins on religion and populism

Onaje X. O. Woodbine on transcendence in sports